W

Bear Lake, Rocky Mountain National Park

Huffer's Hill, above timberline,
Rocky Mountain National Park

WHAT *you* WILL SEE

Georgetown Loop Railroad train on Devil's Gate trestle

Georgetown has 200 preserved buildings and residences

The Ten-Mile Range and Breckenridge
from Boreas Pass Road

Gondola ride, Vail

WHAT *you* WILL SEE

Train depot, South Park City Museum, Fairplay

Diorama of gold miners at work, South Park City Museum

Rafting on the Arkansas River, near Buena Vista

Chalk Creek Canyon, near Buena Vista

WHAT *you* WILL SEE

Stark Brothers General Store,
St. Elmo ghost town

1,053-foot-high Royal Gorge Bridge,
Cañon City

Circa-1878 Hornbek Homestead, Florissant

Cadet Chapel, U.S. Air Force Academy, Colorado Springs

Garden of the Gods, Colorado Springs

Dinner and entertainment, Flying W Ranch, Colorado Springs

Let's Go to Colorado!

■ You want to visit Colorado...but don't know where to go, what to do, or where to eat and sleep.

■ Because we've been there and done that, many times, we've been able to research and plan a great trip for you. The scenery and daily activities don't get any better than this! We've pre-tested everything to ensure your enjoyment.

■ All you need to do is get in the car and follow this guide for seven days/950 miles. Or, if you don't have seven days, you can do half the tour in four days—and come back for the rest when you have time. This is the only resource you'll need, although at the back of the book you'll find resources that may be helpful if you have more than seven days, or if you have other interests.

■ To be honest, we've visited many of the accommodations and restaurants we list here, but not all. The accommodations that we have not visited are consensus recommendations by trustworthy local residents or innkeepers, by the American Automobile Association or Mobil guides, or by Woodall's (for campgrounds). The restaurants listed are consensus selections by local residents or ones we've enjoyed and recommend. If your tastes or budget take you in a different direction, just ask your innkeeper, concierge or front desk person for suggestions.

■ What's the best time to tour Colorado? Any time from July 4 through Labor Day/early September, because that's when all the roads, attractions and museums are open. Wildflowers are best in July. The Aspen trees turn gorgeous yellow from mid-September to early October. There are fewer tourists in spring and fall. Winter is cold, but Colorado is especially beautiful with snow on the mountains.

■ What's it likely to cost? The two of us recently completed this tour for about $2,000, which covered our lodging, food, car rental, gasoline, entrance fees, dog kenneling and film developing. Our lodging, food and car choices were in the moderate range. Airfare was not included.

So, come along; let us be your guides. See why we strongly agree with this advertisement by the State of Colorado: *Scenic Colorado will take your breath away. Adventurous Colorado will challenge you. Relaxing Colorado will soothe you. Historic Colorado will transport you. But it can't happen until you're here!*

Seven-Day Tour Route

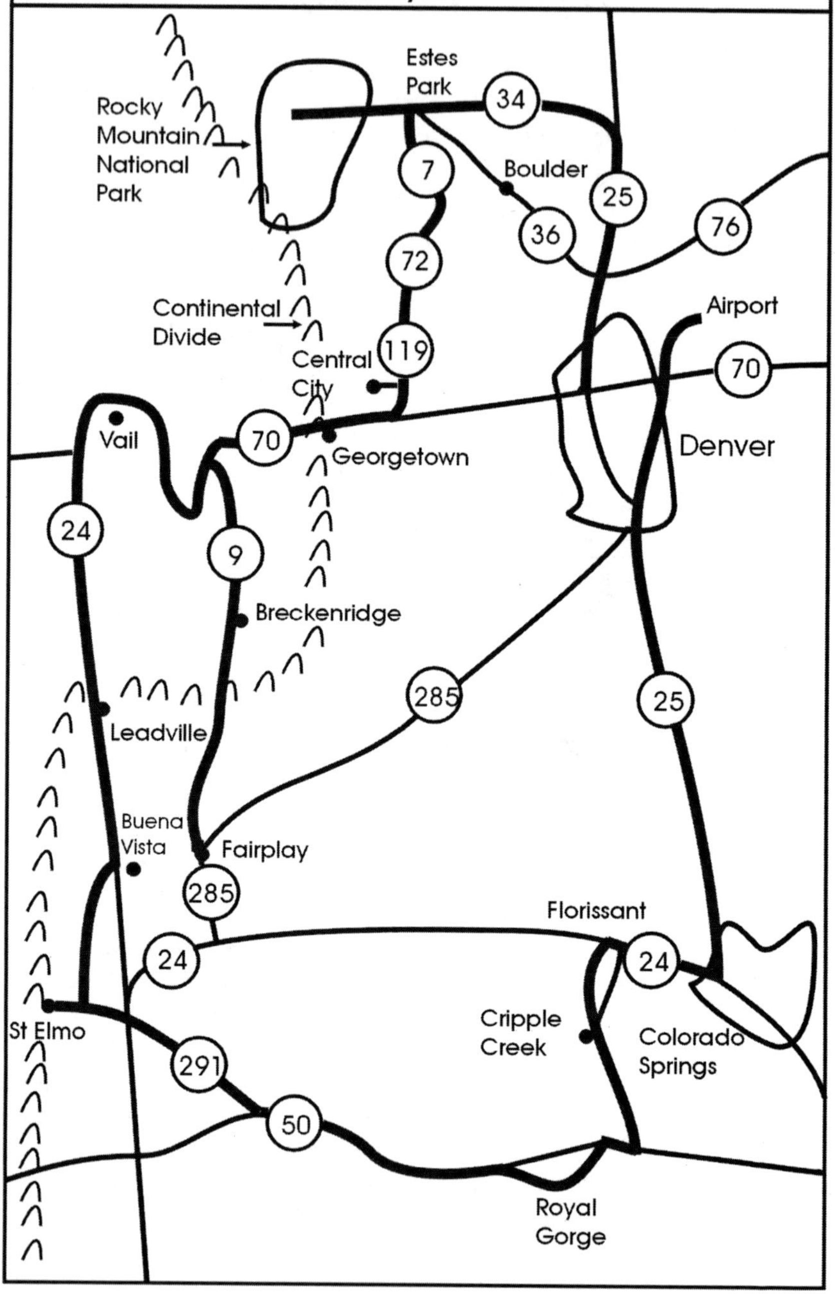

Seven Perfect Days™ Series

Seven Perfect Days™ in Colorado

A Guided Driving Tour

Second Edition

by Bill and Celia Ginnodo

pride PUBLICATIONS INC.

Arlington Heights, Illinois

****

Every effort has been made to provide accurate and up-to-date descriptions in this book. Hazards are noted where known. Users of this book are reminded that they alone are responsible for their own safety when involved in any activity described in this book and that they do so at their own risk.

Substantial discounts are available on bulk quantities of this book when purchased directly from Pride Publications, Inc.

Cover and Photo Pages Design: Philip Ginnodo
Edited by: Joseph J. Ott, Jr.
Maps: K&BW Print Specialties/Bob Webb
Photographs: Bill Ginnodo, except the following photographs by Jeff and Terry Kaul, Arlington Heights, Illinois, with their permission: Bear Lake, Huffer's Hill, Georgetown Loop Railroad, and Royal Gorge Bridge. Front cover photo: Aspen trees in September, near Breckenridge. Back cover photo: Garden of the Gods and Pikes Peak.
Printed in the United States of America by: 360 Digital Books.

The paper used in this publication is acid-free and chlorine-free. It meets the requirements of the American National Standard for Permanence of Paper for Printed Library Materials, ANSI Z39.48-1984.

First published 06/02
Second edition, first printing 03/07; second printing 11/07

Library of Congress Cataloging-in-Publication Data

Ginnodo, Bill.
Seven perfect days in Colorado: a guided driving tour / by Bill and
Celia Ginnodo.—2nd ed.
p. cm. – (Seven perfect days series)
Includes bibliographical references
ISBN 978-0-9656587-3-7
1. Colorado--Tours. 2. Automobile travel--Colorado--Guidebooks. I.
Ginnodo, Celia, 1936- II. Title.
F774.3 .G56 2007
917.9404'54--dc22
Library of Congress Control Number: 2007002192

****

Contents and Highlights

Take a Moment

This is a place
   where you can pause,
Be lifted up
   and calmed down,
Get outside yourself
   and into nature,
Savor beauty
   and experience peace.

So don't just rush
   from place to place:
Don't see everything
   in a blur;
Don't miss the sky,
   the pine bark or cones;
Don't miss the flowers,
   the rocks, the earth.

Take time to touch,
   take time to smell;
Take time to taste,
   take time to hear and really see.
Use all your senses
   to get the feel
Of the wonder and delight
   that is Colorado.

...as when we stood high above Vail, at the edge of a small stand of whispering, fragrant evergreens with a pine cone in hand, admiring the beauty of the mountains...and then rode the gondola down to a delicious lunch in the village.

If you're open to such moments, you, too, will experience times of serenity, invigoration, healing and joy during this tour. And be sure to take time for discovery...do things differently, stay longer, learn what else this wonderful state has to offer.

-- Bill and Celia

Maps and Tour Options

Your primary map, no matter which tour option you choose, is opposite the title page and titled "Seven-Day Tour Route." You'll find other helpful maps throughout the book. We also suggest that you purchase a road map of Colorado at a bookstore (most of the chain bookstores have them), or that you request a free road map and Official State Vacation Guide by calling 1-800-COLORADO or logging onto *www.colorado.com.*

Seven-Day Tour

As shown on the primary map, this tour begins in Denver, takes a circular route through the mountains, and ends a week later in Colorado Springs. Because Colorado Springs is only an hour and a half drive from Denver, you may fly into and out of either airport.

Four-Day Northern Tour

We suggest that you follow the seven-day tour as written, through "Day Four." Then, drive the next morning from Buena Vista to Denver via US 285, or to Colorado Springs via US 24, to catch an afternoon flight.

Four-Day Southern Tour

For this option, we suggest that you fly into Colorado Springs and drive to Buena Vista the afternoon before your tour begins. The next morning, drive from Buena Vista to Fairplay via US 24 and US 285, and pick up the tour at "Day Four."

Create Your Own Tour

If you want to vacation more than a week in Colorado, you can spend additional time in each location, branch off to other parts of the state, or both. Whichever you do, the books listed in "Selected Readings" should be helpful as you plan those additional parts of your trip.

What You Should Know About Costs and Reservations

About Costs

In all locations, we have provided a range of accommodations and restaurants to help you find places that meet your budget and comfort needs. We use the following symbols to indicate relative costs. They are approximate as of the publication of this book.

	Lodging Per Room	Meal Per Person
$	$100 or less	$10 or less
$$	$101-175	$11-20
$$$	$176-300	$21-30
$$$$	$301 and up	$31 and up

About Reservations

We recommend that you make advance-lodging reservations in all locations, in order to ensure the kind of accommodations that you prefer. You can save on lodging costs at many establishments by presenting certain membership cards. Therefore, don't forget to ask for your AAA, AARP or other discounts for which you may be eligible!

If you'd like to look at some lodging choices and make reservations the easy way, just log onto www.pridepublications.com. *There, you'll find links to almost all of the B&Bs, hotels, motels, and campgrounds listed in this book.*

As for restaurants, same-day reservations or walking-in should work in all locations, except for The Fort restaurant in the Denver area and the Flying W Ranch in Colorado Springs.

The Day Before Day One

Since there is a fairly good chance that you'll fly into Denver or Colorado Springs on the morning before the seven-day tour begins, and will want to use the afternoon enjoying the area, we have three options for you to consider.

For details on all the major attractions listed in the three options, see "Alternate Activities" at the end of Day One.

(If you plan to have dinner at The Fort restaurant this evening, we suggest that you call ahead for a reservation. See Option 3 and "It's Dinnertime" on the next page.)

Option 1 - Do you usually seek out museums when you vacation? If so, you'll probably lean toward downtown Denver and visits to one or more of the following, which we will *not* visit on Day One: the Black American West Museum; the Byers-Evans House; the Denver Botanic Gardens; the Molly Brown House Museum; and the United States Mint.

Option 2 - Boulder, 30 miles northwest of Denver on US 36, is recommended if you would enjoy driving through the University of Colorado, strolling along park-like Boulder Creek Path, and shopping at beautiful, pedestrians-only Pearl Street Mall. Other activities include a visit to the Leanin' Tree Museum of Western Art and tours of the National Center for Atmospheric Research and of Celestial Seasonings, the largest herbal tea manufacturer in the United States. Have lunch at either Antica Roma or the Mediterranean restaurant on the Pearl Street Mall.

Option 3 - The map on the following page will help guide you. Have lunch at the Old Capitol Grill, 1122 Washington, in Golden, and tour either Coors, the world's single largest brewery, or the Colorado Railroad Museum. Drive up 19th St./Lookout Mountain Rd. and visit the Buffalo Bill Museum & Grave. Just before you enter Interstate 70, look to the right and you may see the buffalo herd. Drive eight miles south of I-70 on Colorado 74 toward Evergreen and visit the Hiwan Homestead Museum. Drive back toward Denver via Bear Creek Rd., stopping to see Red Rocks Amphitheater, called one of the Seven Wonders of the World because of its acoustics and beauty. Continue on Bear Creek Rd., turn right at the stoplight onto Colorado 8, and have dinner at The Fort restaurant. Drive into Denver via US 285.

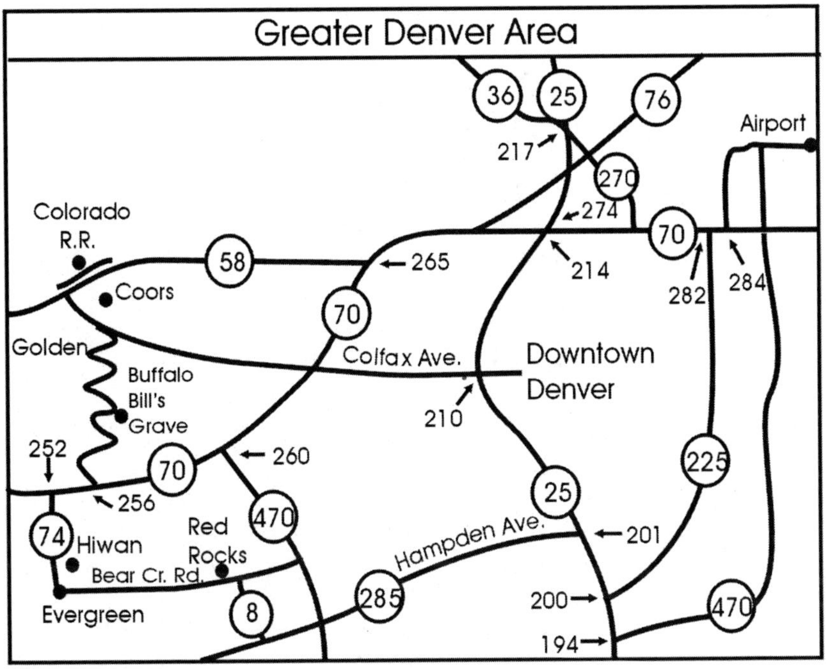

Accommodations

See the listing of bed & breakfasts, hotels/motels and campgrounds at the end of Day One (the next chapter).

It's Dinnertime!

If you want traditional fare, see the list of restaurants at the end of Day One, or simply ask your innkeeper or concierge for dinner recommendations. We have rarely gone wrong doing that, because these folks have had the world's best restaurant critics available to them—the guests who preceded you. Also, most B&B's have a binder or folder of menus that you can view.

However, if you're game for something different, here are some dining choices that are western, entertaining, and ones that we've enjoyed a great deal. We go into detail on these because they are more than good restaurants; they provide a Colorado experience as well as an excellent meal.

The Fort, 19192 Highway 8, Morrison, 303-697-4771, reservations strongly recommended, *www.thefort.com*, $$-$$$$. Even though it's 19 miles from downtown Denver, this is the restaurant we would head for if we had only one evening in the area.

Known nationally for its unusual Rocky Mountain cuisine, The Fort has an ambiance that can't be beat, a panoramic view of Denver, and servers who wear frontier dress. It's a reproduction of Bent's Fort, which was an 1830's-1840's fur trading post 160 miles away in southeastern Colorado near La Junta.

As for the food, it's fashioned after what you would have found in Colorado Territory during the gold-rush days. We usually tend toward different or local fare while on vacation, so we head to The Fort for buffalo, elk, quail, catfish, rattlesnake or The Bowl of the Wife of Kit Carson (a spicy chicken meal-in-a-bowl). Even the ordinary dishes—beef, lamb, pork, chicken, trout, and salmon—are given a western treatment.

Buffalo meat, by the way, tastes a bit sweeter than beef, has less than half the cholesterol and only 2% fat, versus 28% to 34% for comparable beefsteaks.

Along with the usual libations, The Fort serves unusual drinks, such as the authentic 1840 Hailstorm Premiere Julep, Jim Bridger, Bear's Blood, and the Frozen Prickly Pear Margarita. For dessert, try the Negrita, which is an award-winning chocolate- lover's delight.

Buckhorn Exchange, 1000 Osage Street, 303-534-9505. A similar place, serving similar food at similar prices, but in downtown Denver. This circa-1893 restaurant and saloon has memorabilia, artifacts and mounted wildlife hanging from all available wall space; *www.buckhorn.com*, $$-$$$$.

Trail Dust Steak House, just northwest of Denver in Westminster at 9101 Benton Street, 303-427-1446, and southwest in Englewood at 7101 S. Clinton St., 303-790-2420. You'll a find a western ambiance, menu, music, and Country-Western dancing; *www.traildust.com,* $$-$$$.

Day One: The Mile-High City

Native Americans and the French and Spanish explorers called them "The Shining Mountains." Whether seen from a distance with the sun shining on their snowy peaks, or seen from within with moonlight and starlight reflecting from rock and water, the Colorado Rockies exhibit a luminescence and aliveness that those early inhabitants and visitors appreciated. And you will, as well. But let's wait just one more day.

Although the temptation may be strong to immediately head into those shining mountains, we recommend that you literally and figuratively become acclimated to Colorado by spending your first full day and night in the Denver area. There are two reasons for this:

First, touring and sleeping in the "mile-high city" will help get your body used to the thinner air, so you can avoid the effects of altitude sickness later on. (We give you more information about this in the "For Your Health and Safety" appendix.)

Second, we hope to prepare your mind for what you're going to experience during the next six days. As you drive through the gorgeous scenery and explore the historic mining towns, you'll be better able to imagine the wildlife and plant life in their distinct habitats, Native Americans living off the land, and miners working their claims and fighting the elements. That way, you'll "see" more than mountains, valleys, trees and old buildings.

So, delaying your enjoyment of the shining mountains is not punishment. It's enhancement—making the mountain experience even better. Without question, it's what we would do if this were our first trip to Colorado.

Denver Museum of Nature & Science - 2001 Colorado Boulevard; open 9 am to 5 pm daily, except Christmas Day; 303-322-7009, *www.dmns.org.*

We begin our tour here, because it's the only museum that opens before 10 am. If you arrive about 9 o'clock when it opens, that should allow sufficient time to complete the day's itinerary. We believe you'll need two full hours to see the exhibits we've selected for you in this, the fifth-largest natural history museum in the United States.

To get to the museum, drive east on 17th Street about two and one-half miles from downtown, past City Park, to Colorado Boulevard. Then turn left, and left again into the museum's parking lot.

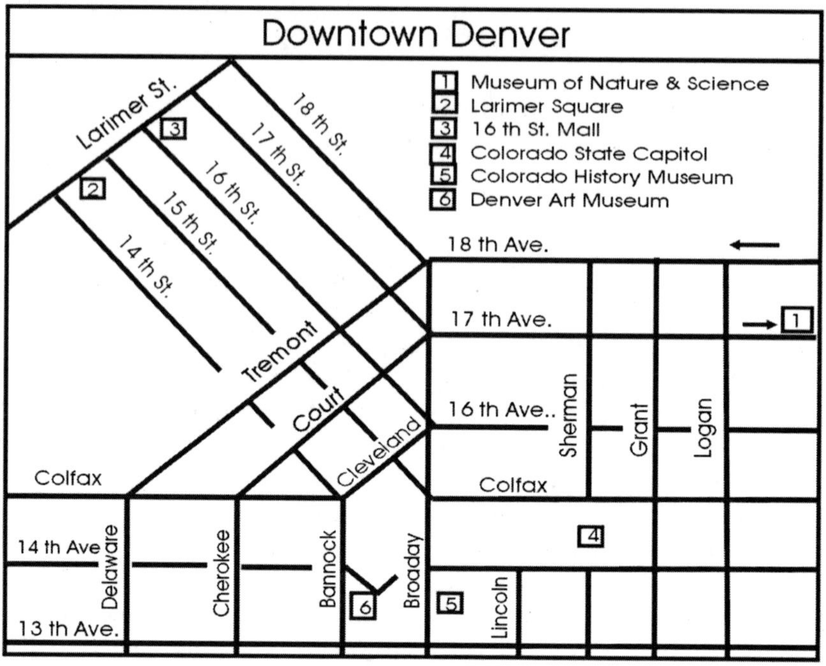

There are exhibits on all three floors of the Denver Museum of Nature & Science that focus on Colorado. We found it best to start with the Prehistoric Journey exhibit and the bird and small animal displays on the third floor, move to the large animal dioramas on the second floor, and finish with the gems and minerals on the first floor.

When you reach the third floor, you'll find the Prehistoric Journey exhibit near the top of the escalator. Here, you'll learn how the earth was formed and how Colorado evolved from ocean floor to tropics to grasslands. You'll also see fossils and skeletons of sea life, insects and dinosaurs found in what is now Colorado. Look especially for the Long-Necked Dinosaur uncovered near the Colorado-Utah border, and for the map that shows how much of the United States and Canada was underwater 95 to 68 million years ago—from the Gulf of Mexico to the Arctic Ocean!

Next, move to Explore Colorado in the center of the third floor. We found these beautiful, full-size dioramas to be of special value, because you not only see indigenous birds, small animals, insects, trees, plants and wildflowers; you see them depicted in the elevations where they live. For example, tomorrow when you stand at the 9,500, 11,000 and 12,500-foot levels in Rocky Mountain National Park, you'll be able to imagine the diversity of wildlife that's generally hidden from view. There will be a richness in those stops along the way that you will not otherwise have.

On the second floor, in the Edge of the Wild exhibit, you'll find more of the museum's exceptionally realistic dioramas. This time, you'll see large Colorado animals in their natural habitats: mule and white tail deer, a mountain lion with cubs, bison, pronghorns, bighorn sheep and wapiti, better known as elk. It's possible that you'll actually see some of these animals during the coming days. We also suggest a quick walk through the North American Wildlife exhibit, where you'll see coyote and beaver dioramas, plus displays of Native American clothing, weapons and various utensils, and an exhibit of mountain men and their beaver traps.

Finally, head for the Gems and Minerals Hall on the first floor. There is so much beauty in the glass cases that you could spend hours studying the tremendous variety of gems and minerals. For our purposes, we suggest that you move quickly through the first three quarters of this exhibit and focus on the section called "Colorado's Economic Minerals." Here, you'll find metals that have been mined in Colorado, including, gold, silver, lead, zinc, copper, pyrite, molybdenite and others. You'll also see old photographs of mining operations, such as those at Cripple Creek (where you'll be on Day Six). You'll be surprised by the various forms in which gold is found, and by Tom's Baby, the largest gold nugget ever found in Colorado. (It's 8-1/2 pounds and located in a side room to the left).

There is so much to see in this museum, including the IMAX movie, that you'll probably find it difficult to disengage yourself after only two hours. But we've got a lot of wonderful things to do during this one day in Denver, so we'll move right along.

We suggest you return to downtown Denver via 17th and 18th Avenues, and that you try to arrive at Larimer Square about 11:30 am to allow enough time for lunch and a good look at Denver's most historic district.

Larimer Square - Larimer Street, between 14th and 15th Streets.

Well, what should we do first....find a restaurant, do some window-shopping or tour the area? Our suggestion, so you don't have to wait in a line for lunch, is to settle into a restaurant and let us regale you with a little historical patter while you wait for your food. Then off to the shops or a brief historical walking tour. All of these restaurants are well recommended by locals. We liked Josephina's very much.

- **Cafe Colore**, Italian, casual, 1512 Larimer St., 303-534-6844, *www.cafecoloredenver.com,* $-$$.
- **Josephina's**, Northern Italian, early 1940's decor, 1433 Larimer St., 303-623-0166, no website, $-$$.
- **The Market**, gourmet fast food deli plus bakery and espresso bar, casual, 1445 Larimer St., 303-534-5140, no website, $.

Now that you're settled, here's the brief history lesson that we promised:

As you'll learn in more detail in a couple of days, the first major gold strike occurred in the mountains west of Denver in 1859, ten years after the California gold rush began. But "color" (flakes of gold that wash downstream from the gold source) had been found in Colorado many years earlier. One such find was near where we are now, at the confluence of the South Platte River and Cherry Creek.

The first organized group of gold seekers, led by Green Russell, came from the State of Georgia in 1858—yes, Georgia has its gold-mining history. They established a camp on the west side of Cherry Creek, calling it Auraria. Soon, another group arrived and drove in their town stakes across the creek, calling the site St. Charles. That group left to register their town site in Leavenworth, Kansas, the territorial capitol. But a third group, led by General William Larimer, "jumped" the claim, naming the town site Denver City, after James Denver, the territorial governor of Kansas.

Auraria and Denver remained rival towns until 1860 when they united and agreed upon the name Denver. By then, there were 25 rough-wood stores on Larimer Street.

Three years later, a fire destroyed the original buildings. Following the dictates of a new building code, all new structures were made of brick...and you can see the result for yourself. Larimer Square was added to the National Register of Historic Places after its restoration in 1973.

Following lunch, walk where Buffalo Bill Cody, Bat Masterson and the early gold miners, gamblers and ladies of the evening walked. Can you imagine the sounds and general hubbub of the saloons, hotels, stores, horses, wagons and people of Larimer Street in its heyday?

If you're interested in a walking tour of Larimer Square, you can pick up a pamphlet at the kiosk next to the Granite Building at the corner of 15th and Larimer.

16th Street Mall

This is a chance to work off some of the calories you just consumed and to do some window-shopping on the way to our next site. So take the 12-block walk (about a mile) down the 16th Street Mall to Broadway and then another two blocks south to the State Capitol building. Or, if you prefer or must, you can hop on one of the free shuttle buses that come by every couple of minutes. Later, we'll be returning to Larimer Square and your car via the mall, so if you'd like to ride the shuttle just for the fun of it, you can do it then.

What you'll find is a treed pedestrian promenade lined with outdoor cafes, renovated historic office buildings, and many shops, restaurants and department stores. The *piece de resistance* of the 16th Street Mall is the Tabor Center, a two-block, glass-enclosed galleria between Larimer and Arapaho Streets that houses 70 specialty shops.

Colorado State Capitol - Enter on Grant St., between 14th and Colfax. Open Monday through Friday, 9 am to 5:30 pm; 303-866-2604; drop-in tours begin at 9 am, noon and 2:30 pm from the first floor reception desk.

You'll notice upon approaching the capitol building that its design is similar to that of the U.S. Capitol in Washington, DC—except that its dome is covered with 24-carat Colorado gold leaf. If you walk up to the fifteenth gray-colored step on the west side of the building, you'll be exactly one mile (5,280 feet) above sea level. This act will validate in your subconscious that you are really in the "mile-high city."

Inside the capitol building, the highlight for us was the observation deck just below the capitol dome. If it's a clear day, and you have the interest, energy and stamina, go to the third floor, where you'll find the staircase. There are 93 steps to climb, and you may find yourself short of breath because of the altitude. But the spectacular panoramic view of the mountains and city is worth the effort. *You should not do this if you have a history of heart or respiratory problems.* An unexpected bonus for us was the interesting display around the rotunda consisting of 16 stained glass portraits and descriptive texts of Colorado's major historical and political figures.

As you leave the capitol building, it would be a good idea to check the time. You have two museums to cover before the Denver Art Museum closes at 5 pm.

Colorado History Museum - 13th Avenue and Broadway; 303-866-3682; open Monday through Saturday, 10 am to 5 pm, Sunday noon to 5 pm, *www.coloradohistory.org.*

To us, this is a special place, one that focuses on the ordinary and extraordinary people who have inhabited and built the State of Colorado: Native Americans, fur traders, pioneers, miners, gamblers, shopkeepers, outlaws, politicians and railroaders.

The best starting point is The Colorado Chronicle, a 150-year timeline display on the lower level, where you'll find the state's history beautifully encapsulated in photographs, news clippings and descriptions. Then, check out the many other displays on that same level, including the very realistic Indian dioramas, Anasaszi cliff dwelling, 19th century Denver, gold rush era log cabin, sod house, mining tools and machinery, and Baby Doe Tabor's $7,000 wedding dress (about $70,000 in today's money). We'll tell you more about her and her multi-millionaire mining baron husband on Day Four.

The museum also houses the Colorado Historical Society, which runs a bookstore on the main level, and is a source of much of the history that's cited in this book.

On the way to the Denver Art Museum, we suggest that you cut through the Denver Public Library, which is just west and across the street from the Colorado History Museum. Go to the fifth floor, where you'll find several wonderful works of art—two Remington sculptures as you exit the elevator, and a wall-size 1877 painting of Estes Park by Albert Bierstadt.

Denver Art Museum – On 13th Avenue, between Broadway and Bannock Sts.; open Tues. and Thurs. 10 am to 5 pm, Wed. and Fri. 10 am to 10 pm, Sat. and Sun. 9 am to 5 pm. Closed Monday. 720-865-5000, *www.denverartmuseum.org.*

As with the Denver Museum of Nature & Science, you could probably keep happily occupied here for a full day. The museum is said to have the world's greatest collection of Native American artwork. It's certainly one of the classiest. You'll find it on the second and third levels. Many of these beautiful artifacts are similar to the clothing and equipment that were used by the Arapaho and Ute tribes of Colorado.

Time permitting, you may want to examine the Art of the American West collection on the seventh floor.

It's Dinnertime!

These western-oriented restaurants were described at the end of the last chapter:

- **The Fort**
- **Buckhorn Exchange**
- **Trail Dust Steak House**

These restaurants you read about earlier today, when you were trying to decide where to eat lunch (dinner prices may be higher):

- **Cafe Colore**
- **Josephina's**
- **The Market**

Here are some additional downtown Denver restaurants:

- **Broker**, steaks and seafood, fine-dining ambiance, 821 17th St., 303-292-5065, *www.thebrokerrestaurant.com*, $$$-$$$$.
- **Cafe Berlin**, German, cozy, 2005 E. 17th Ave., 303-377-5896, $$-$$$.
- **Carmine's on Penn**, family-style Italian, comfortable-candlelit, 92 S. Pennsylvania St., 303-777-6443, $$-$$$$.
- **Sullivan's Steak House**, beef & seafood, fine dining, 1745 Wazee St., 303-295-2664, *www.sullivansteakhouse.com/denver,* $$-$$$$.
- **Wynkoop Brewing Company**, hearty pub fare, brew pub atmosphere, 1634 18th St., 303-297-2700, *www.wynkoop.com*, $$-$$$.

Ginnodo-recommended B&B's

- **The Adagio Bed & Breakfast,** 1430 Race St., Denver 80206, 303-370-6911, 800-533-3241, fax 303-377-5968, *www.adagiobb.com, helen@adagiobb.com*, $-$$$.
- **Capitol Hill Mansion Bed and Breakfast Inn**, 1207 Pennsylvania St., Denver, 80203, 800-839-9329, fax: 303-839-9046 *www.capitol hillmansion.com, info@capitolhillmansion.com;* $$-$$$.
- **The Gregory Inn,** 2500 Arapahoe St., Denver 80205, 303-295-6570, 800-925-6570, fax 303-295-0103, *www.gregoryinn.com, info@ gregoryinn .com,* $$-$$$.
- **The Holiday Chalet,** 1820 E. Colfax Ave., Denver 80218, 303-321-9975, 800-626-4497, fax 303-377-6556, *www.holidaychalet .net, holidaychalet@aol.com*, $-$$.
- **Lumber Baron Inn & Gardens**, 2555 West 37th Ave., Denver, 80211, 303-477-8205, fax 303-477-0269, *www.lumberbaron.com, stay@lumberbaron.com,* $$-$$$.

- **Queen Anne Bed & Breakfast Inn**, 2147-51 Tremont PL, Denver 80205, 303-296-6666, 800-432-4667, fax 303-296-2151, *www.queenannebnb.com*, *travel@queenannebnb.com*, $$-$$$.
- **More B&Bs at** *www.innsofcolorado.org*, and *www.colorado-bnb.com.*

AAA- or Mobil-recommended Motels/Hotels

- **Brown Palace Hotel**, (historic) 321 17th St., Denver 80202, 303-297-3111; 800-321-2599, fax 303-312-5900, *www.brownpalace.com,* $$-$$$.
- **Courtyard Denver Downtown (Marriott)**, 934 16th St., Denver 80202, 303-571-1114, 888-465-4329, fax 303-571-1141, *www.marriott.com*, $$$.
- **Holiday Inn Denver-City Center**, 1450 Glenarm PL 80202, 303-573-1450, 800-holiday, fax 303-572-1113, *www.ichotelsgroup.com,* $$-$$$.
- **The Magnolia Hotel**, 818 17th St., Denver 80202, 303-607-9000, 888-915-1110, Fax: 303-607-0101, *www.themagnoliahotel.com*, $$$-$$$$.
- **The Westin Tabor Center Denver**, 1672 Lawrence St., Denver 80202, 303-572-9100, fax 303-572-7288, *www.starwood.com/westin*, $$$.

Woodall's-recommended RV Parks & Campgrounds

- **Chief Hosa Campground:** Golden; from jct I-70 & US 40, go 8-1/4 mi W on I-70 to Genessee Dr (exit 253), then 100 yards S on Genessee Dr; 303-526-1324.
- **Dakota Ridge RV Park:** Golden; from I-70 & US 40 (exit 262), go 1-1/2 mi W on US 40; 800-398-1625, *www.dakotaridgerv.com, info@dakotaridgerv.com.*
- **Delux RV Park:** Denver; from jct I-25 & I-70, go 2 mi W on I-70 to exit 272, then 3/4 mi N on Federal Blvd; 303-433-0452.
- **Golden Clear Creek RV Park:** Golden; from jct I-70 & US 40 (exit 262), go ¾ mi N on US 40, then 3-1/4 mi W on US 6, then ½ mi E on SR 58, then 3 blocks S on Washington, then ½ mi W on 10th St; 303-278-1437.
- **Golden Terrace South RV Resort:** Golden; from jct I-70 & US 40 (exit 262), go 1-1/2 mi W on US 40; 800-638-6279, *www.rvonthego.com/golden-terrace-south-rv-resort-8htm.*

- **Prospect RV Park:** Wheat Ridge; from jct I-25 & I-70, go 10 mi W on I-70 (Ward Rd. exit 266), then 1 block S on Ward Rd., then 4 blocks E on 44th Ave.; 303-424-4414, *www.prospectrv.com.*

*****

ALTERNATIVE ACTIVITIES

Here are more activities in the greater Denver area to consider. You may choose to do them the afternoon you arrive in Denver (see the preceding Day Before Day One chapter), or you may enjoy them more than those we've selected for Day One. You may find others by consulting the resources listed in the "Selected Readings" appendix.

Free Tours In Boulder

Celestial Seasonings is the largest herbal tea manufacturer in the United States. To get there, drive north on US 36 to Foothills Parkway/Colorado 119, turn right on Jay Rd., then left on Spine Rd.; you'll see the plant on your left.

Each year, more than 80,000 people take advantage of the company's free 45-minute guided tours, given Monday through Saturday at 10 am, 11 am, 12 noon, 1 pm, 2 pm, and 3 pm and Sunday at 11 am, 12 noon, 1 pm, 2 pm, and 3 pm. The tour includes the herb garden, the art gallery, the manufacturing plant and tea tasting. Visitors may have lunch in the company cafeteria Monday through Friday from 11:00 am to 2:00 pm. 303-581-1202, *www.celestialseasonings.com.*

The **Leanin' Tree Museum of Western Art** is just a few blocks away at 6055 Longbow Dr. Greeting card company owner, Ed Trumble, wants to share his world-class western art collection of 300 original paintings and sculptures with the public. Monday through Friday, 8 am to 5 pm, and Saturday and Sunday, 10 am to 5 pm. 303-530-1442, *www.leanintreemuseum.com,* free.

National Center for Atmospheric Research is the other tour we recommend. To get there, drive west on Table Mesa Drive to its end. If you're at all interested in how the earth's weather is created and unfolds, you'll find the center's self-guided tour to be fascinating. The center is open for free tours from 8 am to 5 pm Monday through Friday and 9 am to 4 pm Saturday, Sunday and holidays. 303-497-1174, *http://eo.ucar.edu/visit.*

West of Denver

Buffalo Bill Grave and Museum - 987-1/2 Lookout Mountain Rd., Golden 80401, open daily 9 am to 5 pm from May through October, and 9 am to 4 pm from November through April, (closed Mondays and Christmas Day); 303-526-0747, *www.buffalobill.org, betsy.martinson@ci.denver.co.us*.

A genuine western hero, and showman extraordinaire, William. R. Cody was a phenomenon during his adult life. First a Pony Express rider, then an Indian fighter, army scout, stage coach driver and, of course, buffalo hunter, he gained international fame by taking his Wild West show throughout the United States, Canada and Europe.

The museum is full of memorabilia from his shows, including posters, outfits, firearms and more. In addition, there's a permanent exhibit of Native American artifacts, and exhibits on the Pony Express and life on the frontier.

By the way, you may be wondering why Buffalo Bill's grave is located here instead of in Cody, Wyoming, which was his home. Well, to put it simply, he died here while on a trip and Denver decided to keep him!

Colorado Railroad Museum - 17155 W. 44th Ave., Golden 80403, open daily from 9 am to 5 pm except major holidays (open until 6 pm during June, July and August); 303-279-4591, 800-365-6263, *www.crrm.org, info@crrm.org.*

Here, you'll learn about the history of the narrow gauge and standard gauge steam railroads in Colorado. There are more than 60 old locomotives and cars to see outside in simulated railroad yards. Inside the replica of an 1880 railroad depot, you'll find a model railroad (on the lower level), as well as exhibits with thousands of rare old photographs and artifacts from rail lines that supplied mining camps during Colorado's gold rush.

Coors Brewery - 13th and Ford Streets, Golden 80401, free tours from 10 am to 4 pm daily, Monday through Saturday, 800-642-6116, *www.coors.com.*

The Adolph Coors Brewing Company has been doing its thing here since 1873. It's the world's largest single brewing facility. The free 35-minute tour includes the malting, brewing and packaging processes, and free sampling at the end of the tour. The entire visit takes about an hour and a half. We were especially impressed with the cleanliness and efficiency of the place.

Hiwan Homestead Museum - 4208 S. Timbervale Dr., Evergreen 80439, open Tuesday through Sunday, 11 am to 5 pm June through August, and noon to 5 pm September through May, 303-674-6262, *www.co.jefferson.co.us/openspace* (click on H, then on Hiwan).

This architecturally interesting 17-room log lodge had its beginnings in the 1890's, is beautifully restored, and shows what early mountain summer home living was like.

Mount Evans - Just 40 miles west of Denver. It's possible to drive (and then walk a short distance) to the top of 14,260-ft. Mount Evans on the highest paved auto road in North America. Generally open from Memorial Day to Labor Day. *We strongly recommend against this activity if you have heart or respiratory problems, and that you not do it if there is threatening weather.* Take I-70 west to Idaho Springs Exit 240, then Colorados 103 and 5 south to Mount Evans.

Red Rocks Amphitheater - North of Morrison on Hogback Road, 303-697-6486, *www.redrocksonline.com.*

This is a stunning, 900-seat amphitheater set between 400-foot-high red sandstone formations. The site of frequent summer evening concerts, the amphitheater has nearly perfect acoustics and sits in a spectacular outdoor setting. Free except for performances. Closes at 4 pm on event days.

And In Denver

Black American West Museum - 3091 California St., open Tues. through Sat. 10 am to 5 pm from June 1 to August 31, and until 2 pm the rest of the year except major holidays, 303-292-2566, *www.blackamericanwestmuseum.com.*

Perhaps the country's best collection of historic photographs, artifacts and information about African American cowboys, doctors, teachers, miners, farmers, newspaper reporters, legislators and barbers. Several surprising findings: African Americans constituted nearly one-third of all cowboys and some of the West's earliest millionaires in the Wild West, and families came west in covered wagons and established self-sufficient, all-African American settlements.

Byers-Evans House - 1310 Bannock Street, Denver 80204, Tuesday through Sunday, 11 am to 3 pm, 303-620-4933, *www.colorado history.org.*

Built in 1883 and owned by two prominent Denver families, this Victorian home was restored to the 1912-1924 period and contains original Evans family furnishings.

Denver Botanic Gardens - 1005 York Street, Denver 80206, Sept. 16-Apr 30 open 9 am to 5 pm, May 1-Sept. 15 open 9 am to 8 pm Saturday-Tuesday and 9 am to 5 pm Wednesday-Friday, 720-865-3500, *www. denverbotanicgardens.org.*

Highlights here are the Rock Alpine Garden displaying the many varieties of plants that grow in the mountains, and the other gardens showing the flora common to the desert, plains and foothills. There's also a conservatory that houses 800 tropical and subtropical plant species.

Molly Brown House Museum - 1340 Pennsylvania St., Denver, open daily 10 am to 5 pm June 15 through August 15 and weekends 10 am to 5 pm April through October, 303-832-4092, *www.mollybrownmuseum .com.*

This Victorian home of the "Unsinkable" Molly Brown, who became a national heroine when the Titanic sank in 1912, was built in 1889 and has been restored to its appearance in 1910. It has a large collection of art and antique furnishings. Here, you'll get a good feel for how the upper middle-class lived in the early part of the last century.

The United States Mint - 320 W. Colfax Ave., Denver 90204, guided tours are available on the hour, Monday through Friday, 8 am to 2 pm, excluding federal holidays; admission is free; make reservations online or at 303-405-4761 (or take your chances as a walk-up); *www. usmint.gov.*

If you've never visited one of our country's four mints, here's your opportunity to take an interesting 20-minute walk through a glass-enclosed visitor's gallery and watch some of the mint's annual production of six billion coins being made. There is also a coin exhibit and coin sales.

Day Two: Estes and Rocky Mountain National Park

This day is devoted to scenery and nature study. And it doesn't get any better than this!

What an Entrance to the Rockies!

There are several ways to get to Estes Park.
Our personal preference, and strong recommendation, is to drive north from Denver on Interstate 25 for about 50 miles and 40 minutes to Loveland exit 257B, and then travel west on US 34 through Big Thompson Canyon.

Nothing beats this dramatic entrance to the Front Range of the Rocky Mountains! Three miles from Loveland, you'll be abruptly greeted by 1,500 foot-high sheer walls of gneiss and schist rocks that are nearly two billion years old. This part of the canyon is appropriately called The Narrows. You'll see a stunning example of how a rushing mountain river can cut through rock as it courses rapidly to lower elevations.

After The Narrows, the canyon begins to open up and you'll notice that the lower level rock now alternates with pink and dark red granite. By the time you reach Estes Park, at 7,522 feet above sea level, you'll see mostly rolling hills and mountains of granite, many of which are covered by trees.

And what a magnificent view as you enter Estes Park valley and drive toward town! The full glory of Longs Peak (on the left) and the Continental Divide is right there before you. Now you can see why Rocky Mountain National Park, which straddles the Divide, draws about three million visitors each year.

Estes: A "Parc" Extraordinaire

There are several things about the Estes Park valley that will help you appreciate it even more. The name "Estes" belonged to the area's first white settlers, Joel and Patsy Estes, who came here in 1859.

The word "park" is synonymous with "mountain-enclosed meadow." First called that ("parc") by French trappers, it's nevertheless a very appropriate word for this valley because the main attraction here has always been scenery and recreation.

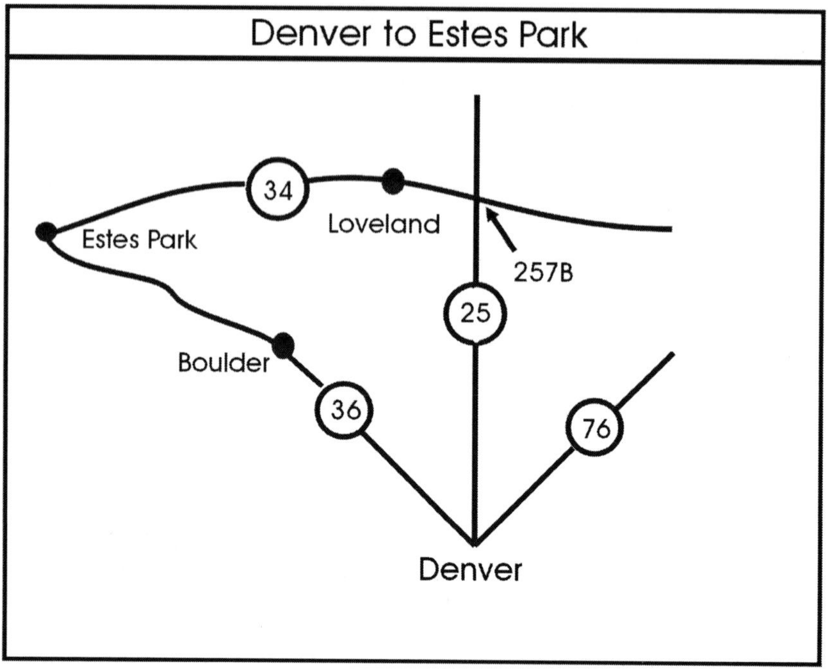
Denver to Estes Park
34
Loveland
Estes Park
257B
25
Boulder
36
76
Denver

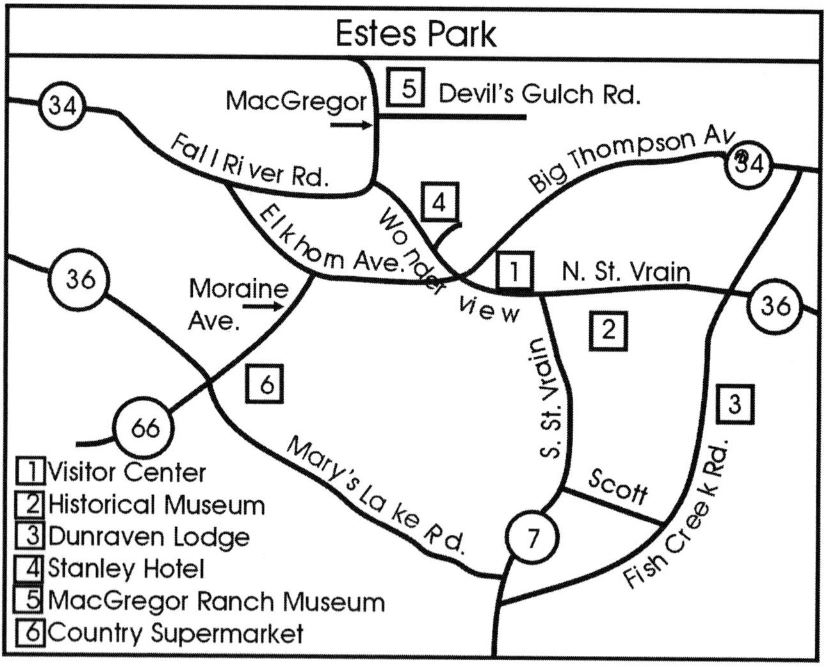
Estes Park
34
MacGregor
5 Devil's Gulch Rd.
Fall River Rd.
Big Thompson Av
34
4
Elkhorn Ave.
Wonder View
1 N. St. Vrain
36
Moraine Ave.
36
2
6
S. St. Vrain
3
66
Scott
Fish Creek Rd.
Mary's Lake Rd.
7
1 Visitor Center
2 Historical Museum
3 Dunraven Lodge
4 Stanley Hotel
5 MacGregor Ranch Museum
6 Country Supermarket

As you approach the west end of Lake Estes and the junction of US 34 and US 36, you'll see the Estes Park Information Center on your left. You may wish to stop there to pick up a few pamphlets and consider alternatives to what we've planned for you. We encourage you to pursue other activities whenever you find them to be more interesting or enjoyable, and to spend additional time in locations, like Estes Park, that are loaded with things to do. The Information Center is open 8 am to 8 pm during summer and 9 am to 5 pm during winter, 800-44-ESTES, *www.estesparkresort.com.*

From the Information Center, continue to the traffic light and turn left onto N. St. Vrain/US 36. About 0.7 mile farther on, you'll see the Estes Park Area Historical Museum on your right at 200 4th St. If you have a keen interest in history, a brief stop here will enhance your appreciation of the area. Or, you may choose to use this time for later browsing of Estes Park's fine array of shops.

What you'll see in the Historical Museum are old photographs and displays about the early settlers, a 1909 Stanley Steamer automobile, a homestead cabin and the original headquarters building for Rocky Mountain National Park. Look especially for items connected with Joel and Patsy Estes, Isabella Bird, Rocky Mountain Jim Nugent, Griffeth Evans, Alexander MacGregor, Lord Dunraven and F. O. Stanley. The museum is open May through October, Monday through Saturday, 10 am to 5 pm and Sunday 1 pm to 5 pm, and November through April, Friday-Saturday 10 am to 5 pm and Sunday 1-5 pm. 970-586-6256, *www.estesnet.com/museum*, admission is free.

After the Historical Museum, continue east on N. St. Vrain/36 about 0.7 mile and turn right on Fish Creek Road. This is the approximate site of the original Estes homestead. Look around; you can see why the Ohio farmer and prospector chose this place to settle!

About 0.7 mile south on Fish Creek Road, you'll see a driveway with a mailbox and wagon wheel on your left, and, largely hidden by the trees, a low, brown-sided structure with green trim. This is an historic lodge that's unknown to most Estes Park visitors and even to many local residents. It's the privately owned Dunraven Lodge, the original hunting lodge of the Fourth Earl of Dunraven.

Dunraven was an Irish nobleman who illegally acquired 15,000 acres of Estes Park land in the early 1870's as his private sporting preserve. Why "illegally"? Because non-citizens were not permitted to obtain land grants under the Homestead Act of 1862, Dunraven "purchased" the land from individuals, alive and dead, who held only temporary ownership. This became a major source of contention between Dunraven and the bona fide settlers, among whom were Alexander MacGregor (whose homestead we'll visit shortly) and "Rocky Mountain Jim" Nugent.

Nugent, a well known colorful character and mountain guide, was allegedly murdered in 1874 by his friend, Griff Evans, at the behest of the Dunraven interests, because he had become a thorn in their side. At least that's what Nugent claimed from his deathbed.

As we continue down Fish Creek Road, plan to turn right at the third street, which is Scott Avenue, but look ahead at the two mountains sitting shoulder-to-shoulder. The one on the left is Mount Meeker; the one on the right is 14,255-ft. Longs Peak. We'll point them out again from the front deck of the Stanley Hotel in a little while.

When you reach the end of Scott Ave., turn right onto Colorado 7 and drive a mile and a half back to US 36. From there, turn left, drive through the US 34/US 36 Junction onto Wonderview Drive, pass the side of the shopping center, and take the first right into the Stanley Hotel, *www.stanleyhotel.com*. If you're not staying at the Stanley tonight, you'll want to spend a few minutes looking over this beautiful, grand old hotel.

Stanley Steamer inventor, Freelan O. Stanley, who with his partner purchased about half of Lord Dunraven's land when it was sold in 1907, built the Stanley as a resort in 1909. Stanley's hotel became a major draw for visitors in the early 1900's, facilitated by the caravanning of twelve-passenger Stanley Steamers that traveled daily to the train depots in Loveland, Lyons and Longmont to pick up and deposit guests. Would you believe that the Steamers carried telephones that could be attached to telephone wires in the event a car broke down?

After you've explored the first floor of the hotel (Dunraven's portrait is to the left of the front desk) and the museum in the basement, walk to the parapet overlooking the swimming pool and simply soak in the exceptional view of the Continental Divide from here. Look closely at the left side of Longs Peak. Between Meeker and Longs, you'll see a rock formation that looks like a beaver climbing toward the summit. That natural monument to their trade must have amused the early trappers.

Next, return to Wonderview Drive, where you'll turn right and then right again, at the Devil's Gulch-Glenhaven sign, onto MacGregor Ave. Just before the road makes a sharp turn to the right, you'll see the entrance to the MacGregor Ranch Museum, *www.macgregorranch.org*. That ridge of lumpy-looking granite mountains in the background is called, appropriately, Lumpy Ridge. What a backdrop for a homestead that was begun in 1870!

MacGregor was a lawyer who helped lead the fight against Lord Dunraven. He also built a toll road connecting Lyons and Estes Park. The MacGregor place is rather unique, we think, because it's still a working cattle ranch that uses equipment from the late 1800's. You'll see some of that equipment, in the fields or around the barns, as well as furniture and other items in the house dating from the same period. The museum is open Tuesday through Saturday, 11 am to 5 pm, Memorial Day through Labor Day.

Now, let's retrace our route and head back to town, where we'll do a little browsing in Estes Park's nice assortment of shops. They're touristy, though not junky, and probably crowded, but you're sure to find some that appeal to you. The MacDonald Book Shop at 152 Elkhorn is one of our favorites.

By now, you should be ready for lunch. In the interest of time, we suggest that you get a picnic lunch and eat it while we have a nature lesson inside Rocky Mountain National Park. We recommend the delicatessen/meat counter located in the **Country Supermarket** for excellent sandwiches to go. You'll find it by driving 1.6 miles southwest from town on US 36/Moraine Ave. to the traffic light at Mary's Lake Road. It's in the National Park Village strip mall on your left behind the Conoco gas station.

Now, let's take the drive that we said will knock your socks off. Altogether, it's 53 miles long and will take about four hours, including frequent stops for scenery gawking, picture taking and close-up looks at the plant life and, hopefully, wildlife. Be sure to have rain gear and a coat or heavy sweater handy; sudden afternoon rain showers are common, and it can be cool at the higher elevations in the summer. Also, make sure you have enough gasoline in the car; there are no service stations in Rocky Mountain National Park.

If you're concerned about the weather, telephone 970-586-1333 for a recorded report about current conditions. The park's general information number is 970-586-1206. Dial 911 or 970-586-1203 for emergencies. The park's website is *http://nps.gov*, which links to Rocky Mountain National Park.

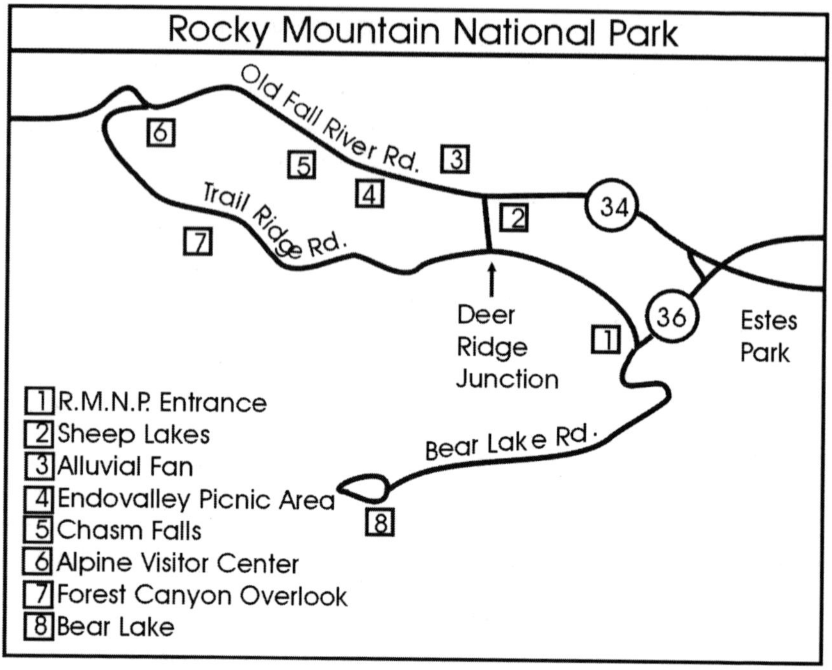

Fall River Road: Everything You Always Wanted to Know About Mountain Ecosystems But Didn't Know You Should Ask

From the Country Supermarket, continue west on US 36 to the Visitor's Center, which is on the left, about three quarters of a mile past the junction of US 36 and Colorado 66. Here, we suggest that you purchase copies of two booklets that are a necessity if you want to fully appreciate the ride ahead. They are *Old Fall River Road* and *Bear Lake Nature Trail*.

Then proceed to the Beaver Meadows Entrance to Rocky Mountain National Park. When you pay the entrance fee, you'll receive a copy of the Trail Ridge Road Guide, which will be helpful during your descent. (If you're over 62 and likely to visit more national parks, ask about the Golden Age Passport; this will also save you money this time.)

Then drive three miles to Deer Ridge Junction, where you'll turn right and drive another two miles to the "T," which is the junction of US 34/Fall River Road and Old Fall River Road. Bear right on US 34 and drive a half mile to Sheep Lakes overlook where it's common to see bighorn sheep licking mineral salt in the mud.

Next, reverse your direction and drive past the "T" three-quarters of a mile on Old Fall River Road to the Alluvial Fan. It was here on July 15, 1982 that rocks and other debris were deposited—44 feet deep!—in a delta shape after Lawn Lake Dam burst and a flash flood carried them in a 35-foot-high wall of water down Roaring River.

(Old Fall River Road opens about July 4 every year. If you are touring before that date, you may need to return to Deer Ridge Junction and drive up Trail Ridge Road, instead.)

Continue two miles up Fall River Road to Endovalley Picnic Area. A very drivable gravel road, Old Fall River Road was dedicated in 1920 and made one-way after Trail Ridge Road was opened in 1932.

While eating lunch in the Endovalley Picnic area, let's consider some of the things we're going to see as we ascend Old Fall River Road.

Rocky Mountain National Park's geography, plants and animals are truly impressive. Here are some numbers on RMNP which should help convince you: 24-by-15 mile borders, encompassing 415 square miles of spectacular scenery; 113 named mountains; 68 mountains more than 12,000 feet above sea level and 17 over 13,000 feet; an elevation range from 7,630 to 14,255 feet (Longs Peak); 150 lakes; 355 miles of hiking trails; approximately 25 mammal and 250 bird species, and 900 species of plants.

To us, the most interesting phenomenon about mountains in general, is that the life zones, or ecosystems, are stacked one upon the other, much like a layer cake. We'll begin our ascent here in Endovalley, which is in the upper montane at 8,558 feet (more than 1,000 feet higher than Estes Park), and will finish at the Alpine Visitor's Center, which is in the alpine tundra at 11,796 feet. In between, we'll drive through the subalpine life zone and an area of stunted and crooked trees called the "krummholz." The life zones, and the most common plants and animals found in each, are depicted on the following pages.

As we climb in elevation, we'll experience several changes that are fun to anticipate. The first is a change in climate. Scientists tell us that ascending 1,000 feet in elevation is equivalent to driving 300 miles north. Since Denver is at 5,280 feet, and the highest point we'll reach is 12,183 feet, our total elevation gain for today's drive is 6,903 feet. That's like driving 2,300 miles to northern Canada...which would put us at the Arctic Circle! That explains the treeless environment, which we'll see when we get to the top of our drive.

Mountain Life Zones

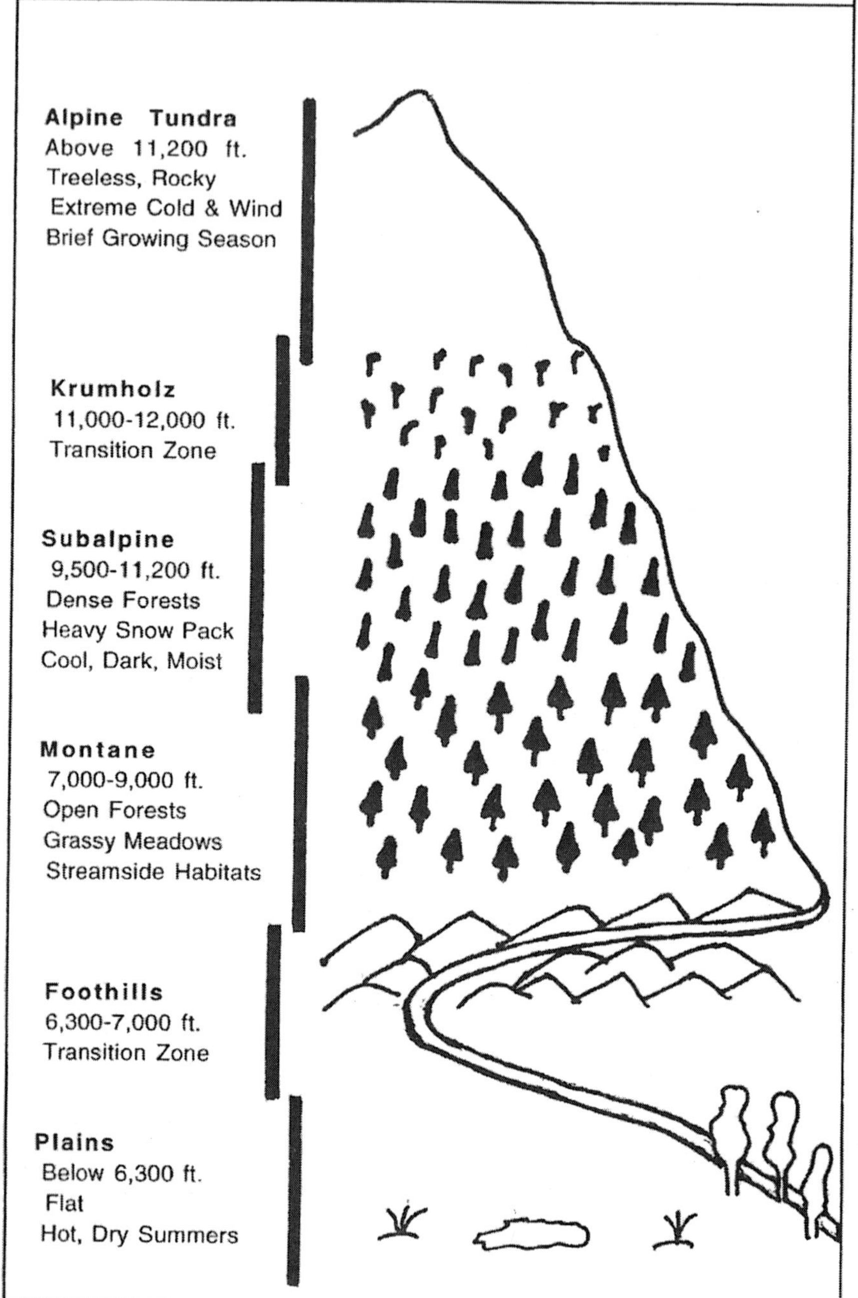

Plants	Animals	
Alpine Aven Old-man-of-the-mountain Western Yellow Paintbrush Sky Pilot Bistort Whiproot Clover Alpine Forget-me-not Arctic Willow Moss Campion	Yellow-bellied Marmot Pika Pocket Gopher White-tailed Ptarmigan Golden Eagle, Hawks, Raven, Pipit, Rosy Finch (summer)	
Stunted pine, fir and spruce	Elk, Bighorn Sheep, Mule Deer (summer)	
Subalpine Fir Engleman Spruce Lodgepole Pine Limber Pine Colorado Columbine Elephantella	Snowshoe Hare Weasel Porcupine	Clark's Nutcracker Graysjay Chickadee Water Ouzel
Ponderosa Pine Douglas Fir Colorado Blue Spruce Aspen Thinleaf Alder Rocky Mountain Maple Indian Paintbrush	Bighorn Sheep Elk/Waipiti Mule Deer Mountain Lion Coyote Beaver Albert's Squirrel Chipmunk Cottontail Rabbit	Broad-tailed Hummingbird Mountain Bluebird Redtailed Hawk Mallard Downey Woodpecker Steller's Jay
Piñon Pine Gamble Oak Rocky Mountain Juniper	Mule Deer Colorado Chipmunk	Magpie Scrub Jay
Cottonwood Willow Sage Yucca Grasses	Prairie Dog Pronghorn Antelope Meadowlark Lark Bunting	

The second change that we'll experience is a change in temperature. The air will become approximately 3.2 degrees cooler for every 1,000 feet we climb. That makes the Alpine Visitor's Center about 22 degrees cooler than Denver.

The third change is in air density as we climb in elevation. It's almost twice as thin above timberline as it is at sea level. That's why you've been a little short of breath, and why you'll huff and puff and have a more rapid heartbeat if you exert yourself, especially during our hike at the Visitor's Center when we get to the top.

So, what do you think; should we take a look at this layer cake now?

Not yet, you say? You want to know more about the trees and how to tell them apart? We're glad you asked!

The first time we visited this picnic area, we asked the same question. We knew how to identify aspens, but the evergreen trees all looked alike; they were just a pretty green blur. So the next time we came, we brought along Vickey and Jim Trammell, botanists who teach at Arapaho Community College in Littleton, Colorado, and paid closer attention to the literature that we obtained at the Alpine Visitor's Center.

The chart on the next page summarizes what we learned. With it, you should be able to take a walk around the picnic area and identify most of the trees. That done, you'll be better prepared for the drive ahead.

Then, let's take that drive, keeping a sharp lookout for the changes in life zones and the wildlife and plant life within them. Do you remember those displays and dioramas in the Denver Museum of Nature and Science? From seeing them, and with the help of the descriptions and drawings in the *Old Fall River Road* booklet and the *Trail Ridge Road Guide*, you should be able to recognize the animals and birds you'll see. Mountain wildflowers are a particular delight to us; there's a good chance you'll see red Indian paintbrush, golden banner, daisies, larkspur and Colorado blue columbine, which is the state flower.

We suggest you turn off your air conditioner so your car doesn't overheat. Take your time. Stop frequently. Let your eyes explore this wonderful, glacier-carved canyon. Discover its riches for yourself. Don't miss Chasm Falls. It's 1.4 miles from Endovalley and is one of our favorite stops because it's there that we've seen the water ouzel, or American dipper, dive into the water to get its food from the bottom of the rushing stream.

Ginnodo's Handy-Dandy, Rocky Mountain National Park, Evergreen Tree Identification System

<table>
<tr><td rowspan="3">Squarish top

Trunk visible</td><td rowspan="3">Long, sharp needles</td><td>2 needles per bundle</td><td>Lodgepole pine (straight trunk)</td></tr>
<tr><td>2-3 needles per bundle</td><td>Ponderosa pine (reddish-brown, scaly bark)</td></tr>
<tr><td>5 needles per bundle</td><td>Limber pine (short, bushy form with long cones)</td></tr>
<tr><td rowspan="4">Pointed top

Branches grow to ground</td><td colspan="2" rowspan="2">Short, squarish, stiff, sharp needles</td><td>Blue spruce (near streams; large cones)</td></tr>
<tr><td>Engleman spruce (subalpine; smaller cones)</td></tr>
<tr><td colspan="2" rowspan="2">Short, flat, flexible ("friendly") needles</td><td>Douglas fir (montane; cones hang)</td></tr>
<tr><td>Subalpine fir (cones upright on top branches)</td></tr>
</table>

On the "Roof of the Rockies"

The Alpine Visitor's Center has an excellent exhibit explaining life on the tundra, which will help you better understand what you'll experience first-hand during our walk in a few minutes. Look especially for the displays covering climate, landscape, plants, animals and birds. You'll also see how several Ute Indian trails crossed through this area.

Outside the Visitor's Center, you'll want to look down into Fall River Canyon. There you'll be standing on top of what's known as a "cirque," a bowl-like depression that was once the top of the Fall River Glacier. Elk are frequently seen feeding among the willow bushes in the cirque; we saw five there on our last visit.

If you turn around and look upward, you'll see the "Huffer's Hill" trail which begins at the edge of the parking lot. (See the photograph at the beginning of this book.) The hill tops out at 12,003 ft. elevation and is a good vantage point for viewing elk in the near distance. *If you have a history of heart or respiratory problems, we recommend that you skip this climb.* Any exertion at this elevation brings shortness of breath and a more rapid heartbeat, even for completely healthy people. So, no matter what your age or physical condition, walk slowly up hill and take frequent rests!

As for the health of plant life, it's extremely fragile and takes many years to repair itself; so for its sake, please stay on the path. If you've come during late June or early July, you'll have the fun of seeing the great variety of miniature wildflowers that bloom during the tundra's very short (six- to ten-week) growing season.

One thing that we found particularly interesting here was the rocks we saw lying randomly on top of the ground. You know they didn't fall from the sky, and that they weren't brought up here by visitors...right? When we asked the Trammells, they said the rocks were literally squeezed out of the earth by the constant freezing and thawing of the moist soil.

At the top of the rise, you can look around 360 degrees and say hereafter that you've truly been on top of a mountain. If you want another top-of-the-mountain experience when you get to Colorado Springs, we provide information in Day Seven on how to get to the top of Pikes Peak.

Isn't it amazing how much of the tops of these mountains are covered with plant life? The word "tundra" means treeless, not lifeless. One third of Rocky Mountain National Park is tundra, and was a major reason why these peaks and valleys were set aside in 1915 as a national park following a ten year campaign led by naturalist, writer and conservationist, Enos Mills.

From the Alpine Visitor's Center we'll take Trail Ridge Road back toward Estes Park, the first part of which is an 11-mile drive along the "Roof of the Rockies." First opened in 1932, this is known as the highest continuous paved road in the United States. It's open from about Memorial Day until heavy snowfalls, sometime between late September and mid-November. The highest point on the road is 12,183 feet.

Here's something for you to consider if you haven't driven much in the mountains: shifting to a lower gear as you descend will help you avoid burning out your car's brakes.

Be sure to stop at the Forest Canyon Overlook where you'll have an even better look into a glaciated valley than at Fall River Canyon (2,500 feet down!). It's hard to imagine, but the ice was about 1,500 feet thick in these canyons when the glaciers were dominant until about 7,500 years ago. Yes, there are still glaciers in the park, five of them, but they're small and inaccessible by road.

Before the glaciers, these canyons were V-shaped as a result of stream erosion. When the ice piled up and gravity pulled it downhill, the glaciers gouged the rock from the sides of the canyons, making them U-shaped. The dislodged rock, which became embedded in the glaciers and contributed to the gouging action, was deposited in long, hill-like formations called "moraines" when the ice melted. You'll have to look closely to see them because they're now covered with trees and other vegetation. We'll pass by a moraine in a little while when we drive up Bear Lake Road through Moraine Park.

The lakes you see below are home to several dozen of the park's black bears, which generally stay hidden from humans.

How about that 20-mile-long view of the Continental Divide from here! Isn't it spectacular? If you'd like to know the names of the peaks, you can consult the chart on the lookout platform.

Have you wondered how the Continental Divide got that name? It's because moisture which falls on the western side eventually finds its way to the Pacific Ocean, and moisture deposited on the eastern side ends up in the Atlantic. This is where the Colorado River begins its 1,400-mile journey to the Gulf of California, which empties into the Pacific.

Another phenomenon that's interesting and incredible to contemplate is that the tops of the mountains along the Divide, and the ground on which you now stand, were under the sea about 65 million years ago, and pushed up to their current elevations when the earth's plates collided in this part of the continent.

Before we move on, look around carefully and listen. It's common to see several species of birds and small animals in these locations. We've never failed to see a Clark's nutcracker, a gray and white bird with black wings that begs for food wherever there are people. And we've frequently seen ravens, falcons and golden eagles flying nearby.

If you're from the eastern part of the United States, you'll probably recognize the yellow-bellied marmot, because it looks like a woodchuck. Its behavior is in sharp contrast to the pika, whose squeak will lead you to the animal itself. A member of the rabbit family, with short, broad ears, the pika doesn't hibernate and is constantly gathering hay for its winter food supply. The marmot does hibernate and seems to do nothing but eat and sunbathe all day.

OK, let's continue down Trail Ridge Road. About three miles past Deer Ridge Junction, just before the park's Beaver Meadows Entrance, you'll find Bear Lake Road on the right. You can, of course, stop at more of the turnouts as you descend, but it's probably late in the afternoon and we don't want you to miss the hike at Bear Lake.

Bear Lake: A Walk On the Sublime Side

Because of its accessibility, its beautiful natural setting and its outstanding half-mile nature trail, Bear Lake is one of the most popular places to visit in Rocky Mountain National Park. (See the photograph at the beginning of this book.) The crowds can be a deterrent in the summer, but you're arriving late in the day and traffic is heaviest between 10 am and 3 pm on summer days.

The drive to Bear Lake is 10 miles from Trail Ridge Road, through beautiful Moraine Park (you know how it got its name) and then upward into the transition area between the montane and subalpine life zones. Keep a sharp lookout for elk, which are frequently seen feeding in clearings between the trees.

You'll find a shuttle bus parking area half way to Bear Lake at Glacier Basin. There will be a sign saying whether you need to stop and park there; if not, drive on to Bear Lake. Buses depart every 15 to 30 minutes, depending upon the date and time of day. The last bus leaves from Bear Lake at 6 pm.

When you arrive at the Bear Lake parking lot (9,475 feet in elevation, and, yes, there are restrooms here), take out the copy of *Bear Lake Nature Trail* that you purchased and proceed around the lake.

This hike is where it should all come together for you. We promised a day focused on scenery and nature; you'll get both here...in spades! What more can you ask for than a gorgeous alpine lake right up against the Continental Divide, and a guided tour of the park's flora and fauna? It's a fitting end to what we hope has been a beautiful, educational and memorable day...

...Unless, of course, it's still early and you want to take another hike. If that's the case, you're in the right place! You can go in almost any direction and any distance from here. The trailheads in the area are well marked, and your choices are shown on the map inside the *Bear Lake Nature Trail* booklet.

It's Dinnertime!

- **Dunraven Inn**, charbroiled steaks-fish, casual, 2470 State Hwy 66, 970-586-6409, *www.dunraveninn.com*, $-$$$.
- **Dunraven Downtown**, Italian, cafe ambiance, 101 W. Elkhorn Ave., 970-586-3818, $-$$$.

- **Molly B**, varied menu, casual, dinner May-September only, 200 Moraine Ave., 970-586-2766, *www.estesparkmollyb.com*, $-$$.
- **Nicky's Restaurant**, American-Italian-Greek, three menus, 1350 Fall River Road, 970-586-5376, *www.nickysresort.com*, $$-$$$$.
- **Poppy's Pizza & Grill**, pizza-soup-salads-sandwiches, casual-families, 342 E. Elkhorn, 970-586-8282, *www.poppyspizzaand grill.com*, $.
- **Sweet Basilico Cafe**, gourmet Italian, casual, reservations recommended, 401 E. Elkhorn Ave., 970-586-3899, $-$$.
- **Twin Owls Steak House**, steaks-chicken-fish, big log cabin atmosphere, 800 MacGregor Ave., 970-586-9344, *www.black canyoninn.com*, $$-$$$$.

Ginnodo-recommended B&Bs

- **Anniversary Inn B&B**, 1060 Mary's Lake Road, Estes Park 80517, 970-586-6200, fax 970-577-8344, *www.estesinn.com, info@estesinn .com,* $$.
- **Black Dog Inn B&B**, PO Box 4659, 650 S. St. Vrain Ave., Estes Park 80517, 970-586-0374, 866-786-0374, *www.blackdoginn.com, dee@blackdoginn.com,* $$$.
- **Dripping Springs Inn,** 37 Dripping Springs Lane, Estes Park 80515, 970-586-3406, 800-432-7145, fax 970-586-3035, *www.drip pingsprings.com, info@drippingsprings.com,* $$.
- **Eagle Cliff House B&B**, PO Box 4312, 2383 Colorado 66, Estes Park 80517, 970-586-5425, 800-414-0922, *www.eaglecliffhouse .com, nancy_maple@beyondbb.com*, $$.
- **Mountain Valley Home B&B,** 1420 Axminster Ln., Estes Park 80517, 970-586-3100, 800-987-2765, fax 970-586-3107, *www. amountainvalleyhome.com, info@amountainvalleyhome.com,* $$-$$$.
- **Romantic River Song**, PO Box 1910, 1765 Lower Broadview Rd., Estes Park 80517, 970-586-4666, fax 970-577-1336, *www.romantic riversong.com, info@romanticriversong.com*, $$-$$$.
- **Taharaa Mountain Lodge**, PO Box 2586, 3110 S. St. Vrain, Estes Park 80517, 970-577-0098, 800-597-0098, Fax: 970-577-0819, *www.taharaa.com, info@tarahaa.com,* $$$.
- **More B&Bs at** *www.innsofcolorado.org*, and *www.colorado-bnb .com.*

YMCA of the Rockies-Estes Park Center, 2515 Tunnel Rd., Estes Park 80511, 970-586-3341, fax 970-586-6078, 200+ cabins and 450 lodge rooms, especially good for families, *www.ymcarockies.org,* $-$$ in the lodge.

AAA- or Mobil-recommended Motels/Hotels

- **Alpine Trail Ridge Inn**, 927 Moraine Ave., Estes Park 80517, 970-586-4585, 800-223-5023, fax 970-586-6249, *www.alpinetrailridge inn.com*, $-$$.
- **Comfort Inn,** 1450 Big Thompson Ave., Estes Park 80517, 970-586-2358, 800-228-5150, Fax: 970-586-4473, *www.comfortinn .com*, $$-$$$.
- **Lake Estes Inn & Suites**, 1650 Big Thompson Ave., Estes Park 80517, 970-586-3386, 800-332-MTNS, fax 970-586-9000, *www. lakeestes.com*. $-$$.
- **Deer Crest Resort**, 1200 Fall River Rd., Estes Park 80517, 970-586-2324, 800-321-2324, fax 970-586-8693, *www.deercrestresort .com, info@deercrestresort.com*, $$.
- **Holiday Inn Rocky Mountain Park**, PO Box 1468, 101 S. St. Vrain Ave., Estes Park 80517, 970-586-2332, 888-465-4329, fax 970-586-2038, *www.ichotelsgroup.com*, $$-$$$.
- **McGregor Mountain Lodge**, 2815 Fall River Rd., Estes Park 80517, 970-586-3457, 800-835-8439, fax 970-586-4040, *www. mcgregormountainlodge.com, info@mcgregormountainlodge.com,* $$-$$$.
- **The Stanley Hotel** (historic), PO Box 1767, 333 Wonderview Ave., Estes Park 80517, 970-586-3371, 800-976-1377, fax 970-586-4964, *www.stanleyhotel.com, info@stanleyhotel.com,* $$$.

Woodall's-recommended RV Parks & Campgrounds

- **Elk Meadow Lodge & RV Resort:** Estes Park; from jct US 36 & US 34, go 2 mi W on US 36 to CO Hwy 66, then 200 yards on Hwy 66; 800-582-5342, *www.elkmeadowrv.com, info@elkmeadowrv .com.*
- **KOA-Estes Park:** Estes Park; from jct US 36 & US 34, go 2 mi E on US 34; 800-562-1887, *www.estesparkkoa.com.*
- **Manor RV Park & Motel:** Estes Park; from jct US 36 & US 34, go ½ W on US 36 to Mary's Lake Rd. (CR60), then ¼ mi S (CR67E), to Riverside Dr, then ¼ mi E on Riverside Dr; 800-344-3256, *www.manorrvparkandmotel.com, elake2@mindspring.com.*
- **Mary's Lake Campground & RV Park:** Estes Park; from jct US 34 & US 36, go 1/2 mi SE on US 36, then 1-1/2 mi SW on Hwy 7,

then 1-1/2 mi W on Peak View Dr.); 970-586-4411, *www.maryslakecampground.com, maryslake@aol.com.*

- **National Park Retreats Cabins & Campground:** Estes Park; from jct US 36 & US 34, go 4 mi W on US 34 Bypass; 970-586-4563, *www.nationalparkretreats.com*.
- **Paradise RV Park:** Estes Park; from jct US 34/36 & Business US 34, go 1/4 mi W on Business US 34, then 2 mi SW on US 36, then 1/2 mi S on Hwy 66; 970-586-5513, *www.paradiservcolorado.com.*
- **Rocky Mountain National Park (Aspenglo Campground):** Estes Park; from town, go 5 mi W on US 34; 970-586-1206, *www.nps.gov/romo*.
- **Rocky Mountain NP (Glacier Basin Campground:** Estes Park; from town, go 4 mi W on US 36, then 5 mi. S on Bear Lake Rd; 970-586-1206, *www.nps.gov/romo*.
- **Rocky Mountain NP (Moraine Park Museum Campground):** Estes Park; from town, go 4 mi W on US 36, then 1 mi S on Bear Lake Rd; 970-586-1206, *www.nps.gov/romo*.
- **Spruce Lake RV Park:** Estes Park; from jct US 34 & 36, go 1-3/4 mi W on US 36, then 1-1/2 mi SW on Moraine Ave., then 1 block S on Mary's Lake Rd; 970-586-2889, *www.sprucelakerv.com, info@sprucelake rv.com.*
- **Yogi Bear's Jellystone Park of Estes Park:** from jct US 34 & US 36, go 5-1/2 mi S on US 36; 970-586-4230, *www.jellystoneofestes.com.*

Day Three: Heart of the Gold (and Silver) Country

Well, two days have already gone by. How time flies when you're having fun! Earlier, we promised full but unhurried days, focused on nature, recreation and history. We hope you're finding that to be the case.

This day is devoted to visiting three historic mining towns. We believe you'll find them to be very interesting and that you'll begin to understand and appreciate Colorado's mining history. That understanding will deepen even more as the tour progresses.

Our route will take us down beautiful Peak to Peak Highway to Central City, site of Colorado's first major gold strike. Next, we'll drive to Georgetown where we'll ride a narrow-gauge train and take a walking tour of this town full of Victorian homes and buildings. We'll end the day in the mining and ski town of Breckenridge, where we'll have a relaxing meal, do some window-shopping, and spend the night.

The Peak to Peak Highway

If you agreed with our assessment that yesterday's drive through Rocky Mountain National Park was spectacular, we think you'll also agree that the Peak to Peak Highway is one of the most pleasant drives you'll ever experience. Stretching 50 miles between Estes Park and Black Hawk/Central City, this drive has been designated by the State as one of Colorado's 21 Scenic and Historic Byways.

But be careful to follow the map and watch the highway signs. It would be easy to end up in Lyons or Boulder instead of our destination.

Winding through the gently rolling topography of the Roosevelt and Arapaho National Forests at about 8,000 to 9,000 feet elevation, with constant, beautiful vistas of forests, peaks and valleys, one gets the feeling of floating effortlessly through the mountains. Consequently, the hour and a half drive will go by quickly—unless you choose to make one stop that we're about to mention. The stop is very worthwhile, if you have even the slightest interest; but remember, this will take some time away from activities later in the day.

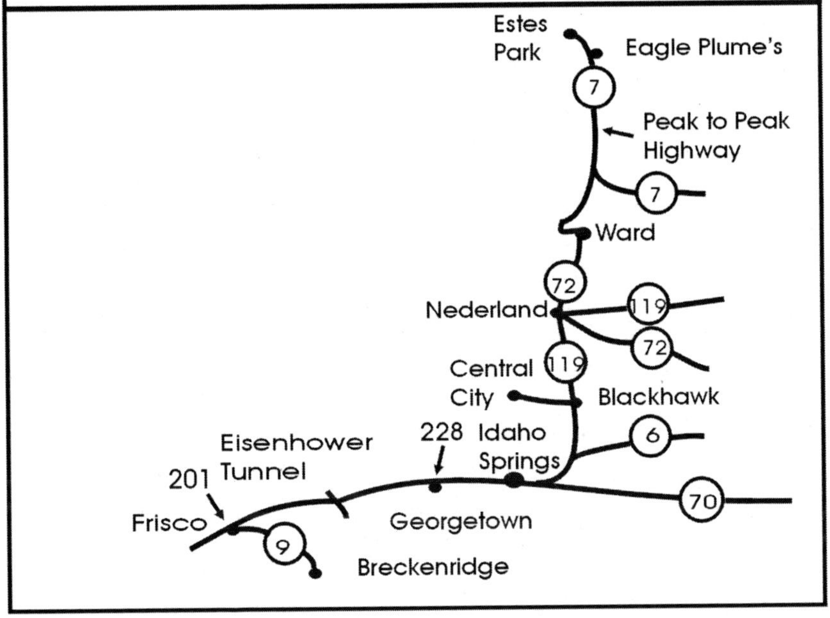

Estes Park to Breckenridge

That stop is 10 miles south of Estes Park, on the left side of the road, just past the sign for the Boulder County Line. Eagle Plume's is part museum, part store and part tourist attraction. We spent 30 minutes happily examining the splendid collection of Native American artifacts and truly fine stock of high-quality, Native American-made goods. It's open daily from 9 am to 5 pm, April through September, and on weekends until Christmas Day, 303-747-2861, *www.eagleplume.com.*

Then, continue toward Ward on Colorados 7 and 72, making sure you turn right and follow 72 when it diverges from Colorado 7. (At this point, you'll be about 19 miles south of Estes Park.) From there, follow Colorado 72 past Ward to Nederland, where you'll pick up Colorado 119, which will take you to Black Hawk and Central City.

Ward is an appropriate place to mention that the Colorado Mineral Belt runs from Ward and Nederland in the north to Telluride in the southwestern part of the state. It's a 50-mile-wide zone that contains most of the state's mineral wealth and mines.

About 65 million years ago when these mountains were being thrust upward, molten gold, silver, lead, copper, zinc, molybdenum, uranium, tungsten and other minerals were forced from the core of the earth through fractured rocks into cracks and fissures that we now call veins.

There are more than 500 known mineral veins in the state's richest region, the Central City-Idaho Springs mining district, which we'll be entering shortly. Most of the known veins in this district have been mined out, but there are many that are very deep or remain undiscovered.

So, you can let your imagination run wild about the hidden wealth that you'll be driving and walking upon!

Central City: "The Richest Square Mile on Earth"

There's a common misconception that an individual named John Gregory first discovered gold in Colorado in early 1859, in a gulch between present-day Black Hawk and Central City. The history of the event is much more complex and interesting than that. Here it is, in brief:

Evidence of gold from five separate locations in Colorado was first reported by Colonel William Gilpen in January of 1849—ten years before Gregory arrived, and the same year the gold rush began in California. But no one paid much attention until repeated discoveries were made by individuals traversing the area, including a Delaware Indian guide named Fall Leaf who carried back evidence to his reservation in eastern Kansas.

That sparked the formation of three prospecting parties which arrived in Colorado during the summer and fall of 1858. In mid-July of that year, a group of 13 men from the Russell Company was the first to discover gold in paying quantities—not in the mountains, but in Dry Creek near the southern limits of present-day Denver.

By December, some 300 people had arrived in the area and began preparing for serious prospecting in the mountains as soon as the spring thaw permitted.

But a 27-year-old Missourian recently-arrived from the California gold diggings, George A. Jackson, decided not to wait and headed up into the mountains. On January 9, he discovered gold in a tributary of Clear Creek near present-day Idaho Springs, and with a group of Chicagoans began panning large amounts of gold. In early May, their secret was out and prospectors began swarming over the area.

On May 6, John H. Gregory, an unemployed miner from Georgia, made his discovery a mountain away in a gulch off the North Fork of Clear Creek. It was here that veins of gold quartz were found for the first time—and the Colorado gold rush was on. Within three months, there were 20,000 miners hard at work in and around Gregory Gulch. Some 50,000 men flooded into the region by the end of the year.

So when you arrive at Black Hawk on the Peak to Peak Highway, turn right and drive one mile up historic Gregory Gulch to Central City, which in its hey-day rivaled Denver in population and as the cultural center of Colorado. What you'll *see* are primarily brick and stone buildings dating from 1873 and 1874, when raging fires destroyed most of the original wooden buildings and homes. What you'll *hear* are slot machines and other gambling-related noises behind the building facades.

Central City and Black Hawk are two of the three towns in which limited stakes gambling was legalized in 1991 by Colorado voters. The third town is Cripple Creek, which we'll visit on Day Six.

If you're just itching to belly-up to a slot machine, or to a blackjack or poker table, you'll do so, of course. But if you can wait a few days until we get to Cripple Creek, we think you'll agree that today will be better spent on the activities that we have planned for you.

In Central City, we suggest that you spend about an hour or so walking around town and visiting at least two historical sites: the Teller House and the Opera House. They're conveniently next door to one another.

The Teller House, 110 Eureka St., a building that survived the 1874 fire because it's made of brick and stone, is both a casino and a hotel. Its notoriety is due largely to "The Face on the Barroom Floor," which has a fanciful tale connected with it, but was actually painted in 1936 by a newspaper illustrator who was attending the summer opera with a lady friend. It's also worth noting that President Ulysses S. Grant, P.T. Barnum, Mark Twain and Mae West slept in the Teller House.

The Central City Opera House, 200 Eureka St., is the town's gem. It was built, with native granite four-feet thick, by the miners in 1878 to ensure that they would have a first-rate cultural life. Early performers included Edwin Booth and Sarah Bernhardt. Except for the years 1910 to 1932, the Opera House has had regular opera performances since its opening. Performances now run from late June through early August (*www.centralcityopera.org*).

Let's move on now to Georgetown, where we'll have lunch and get an even better idea of what it was like to live in a prosperous Colorado mining town in the late 1800's. So, return to the Peak to Peak Highway, turn right, and follow Colorado 119 until it intersects US 6, where you'll turn right at the stoplight. A mile and one-half farther, you'll need to be careful; don't follow the Interstate 70 East signs. You want to continue on US 6 until you reach Interstate 70 West. From there it's just 15 miles on I-70 to Georgetown (exit 228).

Georgetown: "Silver Queen of the Rockies"

The #1 draw here is the Georgetown Loop Railroad. It's a very popular hour-long narrow gauge train ride for adults and kids alike, so we recommend you purchase your tickets before having lunch and taking a walking tour. You'll need to buy them at the Old Georgetown Station, 1106 Rose Street, for Devil's Gate boarding, (Turn right at the stop sign, left across the bridge and left again.) Or you can buy tickets at the boarding area in Silver Plume, just up the highway off I-70. In the interest of time, you can skip the Lebanon Mine tour, because you'll be visiting the much more interesting Mollie Kathleen Mine in Cripple Creek on Day Six.

The Gateway Visitor Center is your next stop. It's at the corner of 15th and Argentine and is open 9 am to 4 pm daily; 303-569-2405, *www.town.georgetown.co.us.* We suggest that you stop there to purchase a copy of *Guide to the Historic District of Georgetown and Silver Plume.* You'll need that booklet, or a substitute, if you are to fully enjoy this afternoon's walking tour.

After the Visitor Center, you may be ready for lunch, so here are several restaurants to choose from that are particularly liked by local residents:

- **Happy Cooker**, American, homey atmosphere, 412 6th St., 303-569-3166, $.
- **Raven Hill Mining Co.**, American/buffalo, eclectic, 612A 6th St., 303-569-2209, $.
- **Red Ram Restaurant & Bar**, Southwest-American, casual-historic, 606 6th St., 303-569-2300, $-$$.

While you're waiting for your meal, here's a short history lesson on Georgetown and its railroad:

The first time we visited Georgetown, we completely missed its significance. We saw only a sleepy old mining town. The train ride was great fun, and the town had wonderful visual appeal, but we didn't look beneath the surface, so had little appreciation for what we were seeing. You won't have that problem, because we're going to share with you what we've learned since then.

Put simply, Georgetown is to Colorado history what Williamsburg, Virginia is to Colonial history. We didn't create that comparison, but we do agree with it. It's a town that's unsullied by new buildings, modern-day commercialism, and distractions such as gambling or skiing. This is the best place to experience what it was like to live in a prosperous Colorado mining town more than 100 years ago. If you look at old photographs of the business district, you'll see that it's virtually the same today. (See the photo at the beginning of this book.) What you'll find outside the business district is a town full of authentic Victorian homes. That adds up to an impressive 200 preserved structures, which will help transport you back to the late 1800's.

The primary reason that 200 of these structures have survived is that, unlike most other mining towns, Georgetown never had a major fire. Credit for that is given to its four volunteer fire companies, whose buildings you'll see as you travel about town.

George and David Griffith were among the first prospectors who arrived in Colorado in the summer and fall of 1858 and positioned themselves for the impending gold rush. But when everyone did rush to Gregory Gulch (Central City) in early May of 1859, the brothers felt they were too late, because by the time they arrived the best claims were taken. So they joined a group of men who prospected west up Clear Creek, past Jackson's Diggings (Idaho Springs), toward the Continental Divide.

George Griffith struck pay dirt on June 17, when he found a gold-bearing quartz outcropping. Other paying lodes were soon discovered and the Griffith mining district, centered in "George's Town," was established. Over the next three years, the Griffiths worked their mine, built a toll road to Central City and hauled in a stamp mill to crush their ore so gold could be separated from the rock. But the gold didn't separate easily and the Griffiths gave up and sold out in the fall of 1862, as did many other miners.

Two years later, everything changed for Georgetown. The miners learned that they had been trying to extract gold from ores that were primarily silver-bearing, and that the town was literally surrounded by rich veins of silver. But even the silver was difficult to extract—until a freed slave from Missouri by the name of Lorenzo Bowman introduced the miners to smelting, a way of converting ore into a fluid state, from which pure silver can be separated. Soon thereafter, a college professor named Nathaniel P. Hill improved the smelting process and Georgetown boomed, growing to 5,000 multinational residents by the time Colorado became a state in 1876. The good times lasted until the silver crash of 1893.

Now, to the railroad. Before the Colorado Central arrived in August of 1877, the transportation of mineral-bearing ores, people, mining equipment, food and other freight was done by pack trains of sturdy burros, horse-drawn wagons and stagecoaches. Those methods of transport were very difficult and expensive, and took a long time. Georgetown needed the railroad to ensure its success and prosperity.

The Colorado Central had even bigger things in mind. The plan was to push on to Silver Plume and to Leadville beyond the Continental Divide. While the line never crossed the Divide, it did reach Silver Plume and go a few miles beyond. But that required an engineering miracle.

Silver Plume, just two miles away, is 638 feet higher in elevation than Georgetown. That was too steep a climb, even for a narrow-gauge railroad. (Such railroads, with their rails three feet apart, were used in mountains where trains needed to negotiate tight curves and steep grades.) A locomotive could not pull railroad cars up a 6 percent grade; a way had to be devised to cut the grade to 3 percent. The solution seemed impossible; such a feat had never been accomplished, anywhere. Finally, the Union Pacific's chief engineer, Jacob B. Blickensderfer, came up with a solution: 4.5 miles of track, three hairpin curves, three bridges, and a 360-degree loop with a high trestle which allowed the railroad to cross over itself and complete the passage between the two towns. The 300-foot long, 95.6 ft.-high trestle was completed in early 1884 across a narrow part of Clear Creek Canyon known as Devil's Gate. (See the photograph at the beginning of this book.)

That done, the railroad soon learned that tourists from around the world wanted to see this "Scenic Wonder of the West." And many thousands did, up to seven trainloads a day! This kept the railroad solvent for another 40 years beyond 1893, when Georgetown's mining fortunes crashed along with the price of silver.

The high bridge was dismantled in 1939, but was rebuilt in 1984 as part of the movement to help people discover what mining and railroads were like more than a century ago. In 1966, the entire Georgetown-Silver Plume mining area was designated as a National Historic Landmark District under the new National Historic Preservation Act.

The Georgetown Loop Railroad is open daily from late May through early October, PO Box 249, Georgetown 80444, 888-456-6777, *www.georgetownlooprr.com, info@railstarusa.com.*

Finished with lunch? Get out that *Guide to the Historic District* you purchased earlier and enjoy! Our favorite structures in Georgetown are the Hotel de Paris and the Hamill House.

The **Hotel de Paris Museum**, 409 6th Street, was personally designed, built and operated from 1875 to 1900 by a mysterious, eccentric and sophisticated Frenchman who called himself Louis Dupuy. The design was influenced by Dupuy's recollection of the inns of his youth in Normandy, France. Wealthy Easterners and Europeans went out of their way to taste Louis' gourmet French cooking and extensive wine cellar, and to enjoy his stimulating discussions about literature, art and philosophy. Look especially at the elegant dining room with its Haviland china, the large and brightly painted kitchen, Louis' extensive book collection, the artwork on the walls, and the original furnishings—including the bed in the salesman's room that folds into a desk. Open daily June through September, 10 am to 4:30 pm; May, and September through December, weekends only, noon to 4 pm; closed January through April; 303-569-2311, *www.hoteldeparis museum.org.*

The **Hamill House**, 305 Argentine Street, is a Country Gothic Revival-style residence that was mostly built between 1874 and 1879 to the specific requirements of William A. Hamill. He was an Englishman who became Georgetown's most famous mine owner-businessman-politician. Three other structures were added to the property between 1880 and 1885: the carriage house and Hamill's office building (both in the Victorian Chateauesque style), and the ornate privy with its separate accommodations for family and servants. In the house itself, you'll especially want to look for the walnut woodwork, imported marble fireplaces, hand-painted wall and ceiling coverings, scrolled hardware, solarium, and antique glass collection. Summer hours: 10 am to 4 pm daily. September through December 25: 12 pm to 4 pm Saturday and Sunday; 303-569-2840, *www.historicgeorgetown.org/houses/hamill.*

Special Note for RVers and Campers

Before you head toward Breckenridge, you should know that there is only one campground in that immediate area that has hookups. (It does have 365 sites with full hookups.) The next closest campgrounds—none have hookups—are in Frisco and Dillon (west on Interstate 70), nine and fourteen miles north of Breckenridge. The next closest campground with hookups is in Idaho Springs, 15 miles east of Georgetown on Interstate 70 (23 sites with hookups). See the campground listings at the end of this chapter.

"The Kingdom of Breckenridge"

To get to Breckenridge, you should drive west on Interstate 70, travel through the Eisenhower Tunnel (under the Continental Divide), turn off at Frisco Exit 203, and drive nine miles south on Colorado 9. That large body of water on your left that you'll see as you approach Dillon and Frisco is the Dillon Reservoir, which provides much-needed water to Denver and environs. Paralleling Colorado 9, on your right as you head south is the very picturesque Tenmile Range, with Frisco at one end and Breckenridge (9,603-foot elevation) at the other. (See the photograph at the beginning of this book.)

Also on your right as you approach Breckenridge, you'll see mounds and mounds of rocks, and you'll want to know what they are. So, we'll tell you.

During the Ice Age, this area was covered by glaciers that gouged gold from these mountainsides and deposited it primarily in the Blue River, the Swan River, and French Gulch. The gold wasn't difficult to find when the first party of prospectors came over the Divide in 1859, and another rush ensued. The precious metal was taken from the streams by panning and other forms of placer mining, and from the hillsides via hard-rock mining and hydraulicking—washing away the hillsides with water which was carried down from higher elevations in flumes and forced through hoses and an 11-foot nozzle called a monitor. (You can see a monitor in front of the Court House on Lincoln Ave.)

Then, between 1898 and 1942, huge gold-dredging boats literally turned several streams in the Breckenridge area upside-down searching for gold that had worked its way down next to the bedrock. No attempt was made to smooth over the damage, so we're all stuck with the resulting eyesore. Fortunately, the beauty of the Tenmile Range and the Blue River Valley is such that you learn to ignore these mounds of rocks. If you want to learn more about the dredging of the Blue River, stop at the historic marker on your right before you enter Breckenridge.

As with Estes Park, Central City, Georgetown and all of Colorado's historic towns, Breckenridge has its own set of interesting stories. There's the one about Tom Groves who found Colorado's largest gold nugget (you saw it in the Denver Museum of Nature and Science) and carried it to town in a blanket, earning for it the nickname "Tom's Baby." And there's Father John Dyer, a Methodist minister who earned the sobriquet "The Snow Shoe Itinerant," because he skied a weekly circuit between gold camps to hold services and deliver mail. You can see the church that he founded in Breckenridge at the corner of Wellington Road and Briar Rose Lane.

Marshall and Martha Silverthorn were beloved by the miners, he for the work he did as the local judge, and she for her kindness to miners when they were down and out.

Barney Ford, a runaway slave, earned a place in local history when he was chased away from his mining claim by white men and bounced back as a restaurant owner and mine investor. Ford Hill, south of town at the beginning of Boreas Pass Road, is named for him.

And, of course, you want to know what the "Kingdom of Breckenridge" is or was. Because of a quirk in the Louisiana Purchase, Breckenridge was within a slice of Colorado that had not been formally acquired from France in 1803. After Breckenridge inhabitants made their argument for independence in 1936, Governor Edwin C. Johnson declared the area to be a part of Colorado, and further declared that Breckenridge could be an independent kingdom for three days every year. There's an annual celebration of this anomaly (in August), as you might guess.

By the way, "Breckenridge" was originally spelled with an "in" instead of an "en." The town was named for Abraham Lincoln's Vice President, John C. Breckinridge, in order to entice the government to establish a post office in the new mining town. Residents changed the spelling when it turned out that Breckinridge sympathized with the Confederacy during the Civil War.

But that's enough history for today. You need to check into your room and have that relaxing dinner we promised. After dinner we'll tell you about some things to do in and around Breckenridge.

It's Dinnertime!

Breckenridge has an abundance of restaurants. These are among the favorites:

- **Breckenridge Brewery**, pub food, bar ambiance, 600 S. Main St., 970-453-1550, *www.breckbrew.com,* $-$$.
- **Cafe Alpine**, American, fine dining, 106 E. Adams St., 970-453-8218, *www.cafealpine.com,* $$.
- **Downstairs at Erics**, burgers & pizza, casual-families-games, 111 S. Main St., 970-453-1401, *www.downstairsaterics.com*, $.
- **Hearthstone Victorian Dining**, American-Coloradan, Victorian ambiance, 130 S. Ridge St., 970-453-1148, *www.hearthstone restaurant.com,* $$$-$$$$.
- **Swiss Haven**, fondue-American, casual, 325 S. Main St., 970-453-6969, no website, $$-$$$$.

If you want to walk off that full feeling after dinner, you're certainly in the right place! Breckenridge has more than 200 shops, restaurants, galleries and bars. Even non-shoppers, like the male half of your guide tandem, can find something to interest them behind those historic and recently constructed Breckenridge facades.

There's a good reason for all those shops: Breckenridge's four interconnected ski mountains and 2,000 acres of ski-able terrain draw more than one million skiers every winter. And many of them spend their evenings browsing and buying. Besides shopping and downhill skiing during the winter, Breckenridge has sleigh riding, guided snowmobile touring and wonderful trails for cross-country skiing, which we've particularly enjoyed.

But, perhaps surprisingly, we think that summer is the time Breckenridge really shines. This may sound like a chamber of commerce ad, but here is a list of things to do when there is no snow on the slopes: hiking on 200 miles of trails; biking on a 40-mile paved path that parallels the Blue River north to Frisco and then circles Dillon Reservoir, or heads west all the way to Vail; backcountry jeep tours and ghost town visits; guided-group walking tours through the historic district; hot-air ballooning; fly fishing; river rafting; mine tours; golf; horseback riding; live theater; and a two-month-long classical music festival.

For pamphlets that describe all of these activities, stop by the Activity Center at 203 S. Main, 970-453-5579, 877-864-0868, *www.gobreck.com*. Look especially for the Vacation Planner and the two Historical Walking Tour pamphlets which will lead you to 48 historic structures, most of which are along Main Street.

Now that you know about Breckenridge's many advantages, you probably wish you'd scheduled more time here. In fact, if we were looking for a Colorado town to use as a summer vacation base—one that would also allow us to take day trips to most of the mountain sites that are included in our tour—this would be the place. Every time we visit Breckenridge, we feel like cats on a beach; there are so many ways to satisfy that urge!

Ginnodo-recommended B&Bs

- **Allaire Timbers Inn**, PO Box 4653, 9511 Hwy. 9, Breckenridge 80424, 970-453-7530, 800-624-4904, fax 970-453-8699, *www.allairetimbers.com, allaire@colorado.net,* $$-$$$.
- **Barn on the River Bed and Breakfast,** PO Box 2454, 303B N. Main St., Breckenridge 80424, 970-453-2975, 800-795-2975, fax 970-453-5258, *www.breckenridge-inn.com*, *info@breckenridge-inn.com*, $$-$$$.
- **Fireside Inn,** (B&B and hostel), PO Box 2252, 114 N. French St., Breckenridge 80424, 970-453-6456, fax 970-453-9577, *www.firesideinn.com, info@firesideinn.com*, $-$$.
- **Four Peaks Inn,** PO Box 1118, 407 S. Ridge St., Breckenridge 80424, 970-453-3813, fax 260-846-3494, *www.fourpeaksinn.com, reservations@fourpeaksinn.com*, $-$$.

- **More B&Bs at** *www.innsofcolorado.org*, and *www.colorado-bnb.com.*

AAA- or Mobil-recommended Motels/Hotels

- **Beaver Run Resort and Conference Center**, PO Box 2115, 620 Village Rd., Breckenridge 80424, 970-453-6000, 800-265-3560, fax 970-453-4284, *www.beaverrun.com, stay@beaverrun.com*, $$-$$$.
- **Great Divide Lodge,** 550 Village Rd., Breckenridge 80424, 970-547-5550, fax 970-453-0212, *http://breckresorts.com/greatdivide,* $$.
- **Pine Ridge Condominiums**, PO Box 487, 400 Four O'Clock Rd., Breckenridge 80424, 970-453-6946, fax 970-453-0746, $119.
- **The Village at Breckenridge Hotel,** PO Box 8329, 535 S. Park Ave., Breckenridge 80424, 970-453-2000, fax 970-453-5116, *http://breckresorts.com/villageatbreckenridge/ $$-$$$*

Woodall's-recommended RV Parks & Campgrounds

- **Cottonwood RV Park:** Idaho Springs; from jct I-70 and Hwy 103 (exit 240), go 1-1/2 mi S on Hwy 103; 303-567-2617.
- **Tiger Run RV Resort:** Breckenridge; 365 sites with full hookups; from jct I-70 & Hwy 9 (exit 203), go 6-1/2 mi S on Hwy 9 to Tiger Run Rd; 970-453-9690, *www.tigerrunresort.com.*
- **White River National Forest:** five campgrounds in Frisco and Dillon, 9 and 14 miles north of Breckenridge; many sites, but none have hookups; 970-468-5400, *http://forestcamping.com/dow/rocky mtn/wr.htm.*

Day Four: Three Times Across the Divide

Today, we'll head south to Fairplay where we'll visit our favorite historical attraction on this driving tour: the most authentic and complete collection of 1880s buildings and artifacts that you'll ever see—one that will help you *feel* what it was like to live in the Old West more than 100 years ago. After that, we'll head to Vail for a spectacular gondola ride, lunch, and a little window-shopping. This afternoon, we'll drive another beautiful Colorado Scenic and Historic Byway on our way to two-mile-high Leadville, where we'll learn some interesting things about mining. And it's there that we'll learn about one of the most interesting characters in Colorado history, H.A.W. Tabor. Then we'll drop down into the Arkansas Valley and spend the night in Buena Vista, where the vista is much better than good. And, yes, as the title of this chapter suggests, we *will* cross the Continental Divide three times today.

The first time will be at Hoosier Pass, just south of Breckenridge. To get there, simply drive south nine miles on Colorado 9. When you arrive at the parking lot at the top of the pass (11,542 feet), you'll see a marker that illustrates the Continental Divide's watershed phenomenon that we mentioned when we were in Rocky Mountain National Park. You might see the marker as a photo opportunity...with you in the picture.

If you're so inclined, you'll want to keep in mind, for your next winter visit to Colorado, that there are some wonderfully scenic hiking and cross-country ski trails up here along the tops of the mountains.

Continuing south another eleven miles, you'll pass through Alma and arrive at South Park City on the outskirts of Fairplay.

South Park City

Our notes about South Park City include the following phrases: "This is great!" "Not to be missed!" "What a treasure!" "We absolutely loved this place!" You may not be so enthusiastic, but we guarantee that you'll learn and see things that will please and surprise you. We continue to be surprised that South Park City isn't better known; but it seems that being in an out-of-the-way location has kept a lot of people from enjoying this jewel of a museum.

Breckenridge to Fairplay and Vail

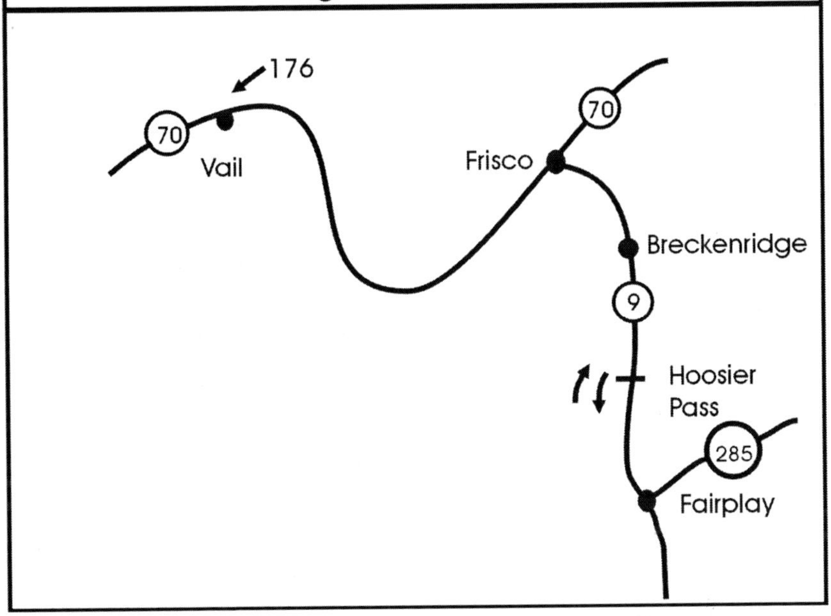

We think that being some distance from the modern hustle and bustle is part of South Park City's appeal. And you don't have to rush about the mountains to see typical mining camp buildings and artifacts...they're all right here!

What you'll see in the next hour and a half or so, are 40 authentic, weathered, mostly one-story buildings from the late 1800s that were brought here from area mining camps and arranged on two sides of a dirt street to simulate an Old West town. Inside the buildings are more than 40,000 original items that were collected and donated by area residents when South Park City was being assembled in 1958. In addition, there is a wealth of other things, such as mining equipment and implements, a narrow-gauge locomotive and caboose, a Conestoga wagon, a cattle-drive-style cook's wagon, a display showing the importance of the burro to early mining operations, and wonderful dioramas in two buildings that show in miniature what it was like to work in and around the mines (see the photograph at the beginning of this book).

We won't tell you about all 40 buildings, because we want you to discover for yourselves what a special place South Park City is. However, we do want to share our favorites:

- The **South Park Brewery** provides a wonderful introduction to late 1800s Colorado with its slide show, dioramas, photographs, Indian arrowhead collection, display of Ute weapons and culture, beaver traps and dam, miner's equipment, lumbering tools, saddles, chaps, etc., etc.
- The **trapper's cabin** takes you back to the 1830's and 1840's when mountain men lived solitary lives while trapping beaver and trading with the Indians.
- The rustic **caboose** delighted Celia because she could see how its icebox, sink, stove, table, and other accommodations, provided a home away from home for the early railroaders.
- The **stagecoach inn** is Bill's favorite, because climbing the creaking stairs to the three bedrooms during his first visit transported him back 100 years. Upstairs, everything is ready for incoming passengers, and downstairs the table is set for ten.
- In the **schoolhouse**, everything is also ready for the fifth grade kids and their teacher who are shown in the 1890 photograph on the wall.
- **Simkin's General Store** is loaded with 100 year-old canned goods, spices, dishes, shoes, buttons, tobacco, blouses, corsets, a Victor talking machine, a pedal sewing machine, a wringer washer and lots of other merchandise of the day.
- And then there's the **transportation shed**, the **train depot** (see the photograph at the beginning of this book), the **carpenter, blacksmith and barber shops**, the **doctor's and dentist's offices**, the **bank**, the **newspaper office**, the **pioneer home**, the **saloon and gambling house**, the old **drug store** with its large collection of patent medicines... you get the idea. Enjoy!

South Park City, PO Box 634, 100 4th St., is open mid-May through mid-October: 9 am to 5 pm May 15 through Memorial Day, 9 am to 7 pm Memorial Day to Labor Day, and 10 am to 6 pm Labor day to closing, 719-836-2387, *www.southparkcity.org.*

Well, it's time to go back to the real world...at least to modern times. So, let's backtrack up Colorado 9, through Breckenridge to Frisco where we'll head west on Interstate 70 to Vail.

What's that you asked? Does coming back over Hoosier Pass count as a second time over the Divide? Yes, it does. We could travel between Fairplay and Breckenridge via Boreas Pass, but that's a long way around, and the road isn't as wide or safe. Maybe, if you're adventurous and on an extended tour....

Back to Interstate 70, where you'll head west, pay particular attention to the scenery between Frisco and Copper Mountain Ski

Resort. This has got to be one of the most gorgeous stretches of interstate highway in the United States, with its steep, dramatic rock walls, trees in abundance and beauty everywhere you look.

Vail and Beyond

When you arrive in the Vail area, take Exit 176 and follow the information and parking signs west to the large parking garage. Then park, exit the southwest corner of the garage, and follow the path around to the right for about 150 yards until you see the Eagle Bahn gondola in LionsHead Village. (Bavarian-style Vail Village is just to the east.) To your right as you approach the gondola is Bart and Yeti's restaurant. That's where we recommend you have lunch today, unless you'd rather eat at the cafeteria or Stube restaurant at the top of the gondola ride, or select another place while you're window shopping.

You now have two tough decisions to make: which to do first, ride the gondola or have lunch; second, what kind of sandwich to have. We selected Bart and Yeti's (970-476-2754 or 1742), because it has outside seating under table umbrellas and is convenient to the gondola. We recommend it because their sandwiches are different and quite delicious. An alternative to Bart and Yeti's is Kaltenberg Castle, which is on the hill just behind the gondola ticket booth, where you can enjoy German food and their own tasty brew, 970-479-1050.

As for the gondola, you'll see that the cars are enclosed and roomy, and that the ride is safe. Of course, this is the primary method of transporting skiers up the mountain during ski season. Hours of operation during the summer are 10 am to 5 pm. Altogether, your ride up and back, including walk-around time while up there, will take about an hour. (See the photograph at the front of this book.)

All we'll say is that the 15-minute ride to the top is smooth and dramatic, the 320-degree view from 10,327 feet is wonderful, and you'll feel like Julie Andrews in the opening scene of "The Sound of Music" as you walk several hundred yards along the path toward the west.

Back on earth—down in LionsHead Village, that is—you may want to take a stroll through this world-famous ski resort. You'll notice that Vail's upscale shopping opportunities are numerous. So if you're more interested in shopping than in the National Mining Hall of Fame and Museum in Leadville, you may just want to hang out here for an hour or so. But if you'd rather keep up with us, let's head for the car!

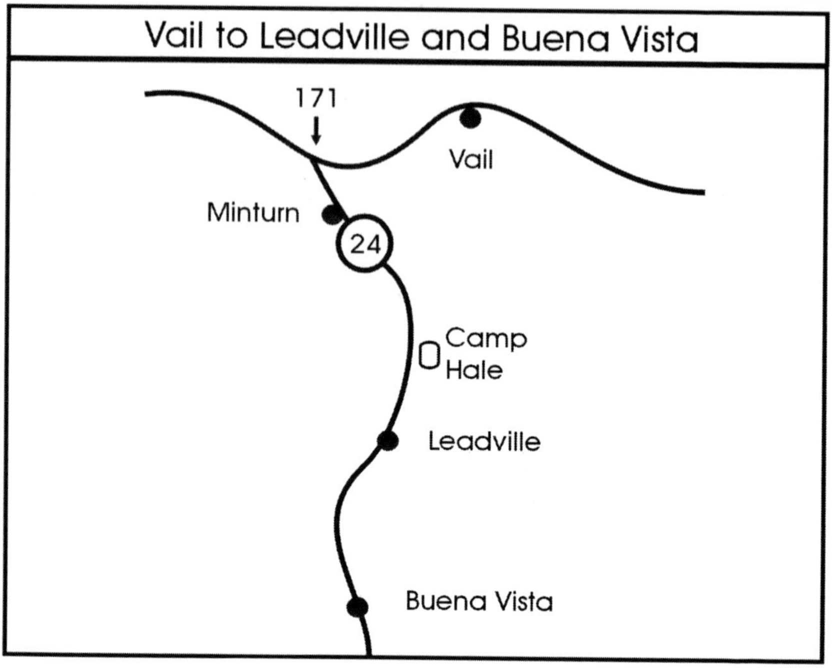

Return to Interstate 70 the way you came, then head west, turn off just a few miles down the road at Minturn Exit 171, and go south on US 24 through Minturn. Make a note of your mileage as you leave Minturn, because there are several sites we want to point out.

The 30-mile stretch of road between Minturn and Leadville is particularly beautiful. It's the upper part of another Colorado Scenic and Historic Byway. The road climbs steeply into the White River National Forest, twists and turns along the Eagle River, and crosses the Continental Divide at Tennessee Pass. We believe you'll agree that the views from the passenger side of the car are breathtaking.

At about five miles from Minturn, you'll come upon an unusual site—an abandoned town called Gilman. The Eagle Mine, once Colorado's major producer of zinc, is located here. It went bankrupt in the late 1980's, and these homes have been vacant ever since.

Then, three miles farther on, be sure to have your camera handy if you like to take bridge pictures.

Fifteen miles from Minturn, you'll come upon the site of Camp Hale, the former headquarters and training ground of the U.S. Army's 10th Mountain Division. Situated in a now-deserted glacial valley, Camp Hale was home to 14,000 men who trained here for battle in the mountains of Europe during World War II. If this interests you even a little bit, we suggest a 10-minute stop at the pullout on your left, to read the interpretive display and imagine what it was like back then.

Six miles later, it's over Tennessee Pass (10,424 feet) and on to Leadville. Yes, this is your third and final time across the Divide today. It's here that the Eagle River, a tributary of the Colorado River, begins and heads north, and the Arkansas River begins and heads south. Of course, rivers don't just begin at a particular spot, unless they're coming from a glacier or an underground water source. It's here that the water runoff from snow and rain funnels into, and creates the beginnings of, these two rivers. We'll be driving beside the Arkansas the remainder of this afternoon and most of tomorrow.

About a mile and a half down from the pass, look to your left and you'll see a picturesque log cabin relic.

Cloud City: Leadville

As you approach Leadville, you'll see the dramatic Sawatch Range in the distance, with a couple of "fourteeners" adding to the spectacle. Sprawling on the right is Mt. Massive, Colorado's second highest peak at 14,421 feet, and on the left is Mt. Elbert, the highest point in Colorado at 14,433 feet. Only Mt. Whitney in California is higher in the contiguous United States.

Situated on the western slope of the Mosquito Range at 10,152 feet elevation, Leadville is nearly a mile higher than the mile-high city of Denver. For this reason, it was often referred to as "Cloud City." This is the highest incorporated city in the United States and at one time had a population of 10,000.

Follow the US 24 signs through town to Harrison Ave., where you'll cross Harrison to 120 W. Ninth Street and find the **National Mining Hall of Fame and Museum**. Here, you'll enjoy a realistic walk-through replica of an underground hardrock mine—important to see if you're claustrophobic and won't want to tour the 1,000-foot-deep Molly Kathleen mine when we get to Cripple Creek. Also very worthwhile are the 21 highly-detailed dioramas depicting the history of gold mining (look for Central City's John Gregory early in the series), the displays of gold, silver, ores, crystals and other minerals, a model railroad layout with trains chugging through an old mining camp, and the museum's art gallery. This federally chartered, non-profit "Smithsonian of Mining" is open from 11 am to 4 pm daily. 719-486-1229, *www.leadville.com/miningmuseum*.

After the National Mining Museum, stop by the Chamber of Commerce at the corner of Harrison and Eighth (719-486-3900, *www.leadvilleusa.com)* to learn whether the Tabor Opera House (308 Harrison, 719-486-8409, *www.taboroperahouse.net, info@taboropera house.net*) is open for tours. We haven't yet been able to tour it ourselves, but we've heard that it's quite special.

Do you need a coffee break or an afternoon snack? We recommend **Cloud City Coffee House** at 711 Harrison. While you're relaxing, here is some interesting history to enjoy:

Like all the towns we're visiting on this tour, Leadville has a unique and colorful past. Its history most closely resembles Georgetown's because gold was discovered first in the area, silver was King here (you'll remember that Georgetown was the "Silver Queen"), and the town's fortunes faded following the silver crash of 1893. The Leadville District yielded more than $500 million in silver, lead, gold, zinc and other minerals.

What appeals to us most about Leadville's history is its most famous citizen, Horace Austin Warner Tabor, generally referred to as H.A.W. His exploits made the Chicago and New York newspapers almost daily and his story has been told often in books, but we especially like the account by Irving Stone in *Men to Match My Mountains.*

H.A.W. Tabor was only one of many people to strike it rich in Leadville. You may recognize some of the others: Meyer Guggenheim, Marshall Field, David May and David Moffat. However, their stories, unlike H.A.W.'s, ended happily.

A 31-year-old former Vermont stonecutter and Kansas farmer, Tabor moved his wife and infant son to the Rockies in 1859 to seek his fortune. It took nearly 19 years, but when he struck it rich, he did it in a big way.

After years of prospecting and running boarding houses and stores, the Tabors were in the right place at the right time. In April 1878, two German shoemakers came into their Oro City grocery store offering one-third ownership of whatever they found in return for a grubstake. (Oro City was renamed "Leadville" for the high lead content of its ore.) Within a month the shoemaker-prospectors had dug down 26 feet to find a silver lode, and before three months had passed, H.A.W. was realizing significant profits from the $8,000 a week in ore being taken from the Little Pittsburgh Mine. By the time two more months passed, Tabor and Denver banker-road builder David Moffat had bought out the two Germans, and H.A.W. owned 50 percent of one of the world's richest mines.

And that was just the beginning. Within a short time Tabor was also part owner of 17 other mines, including the Matchless, and was worth between $8 and 15 million. (Multiply those figures by ten and you'll get some idea of H.A.W.'s fortune in today's dollars!)

Along with the wealth and fame came political and business honors. During his glory ride, H.A.W. was mayor and city treasurer of Leadville, president of the Denver Chamber of Commerce and the Board of Trade, Lieutenant Governor of Colorado, and he was appointed United States Senator from Colorado for a 30-day interim period.

He was enormously popular in Leadville because of his outgoing personality and his generosity. He paid for the construction of a firehouse, the town's public hall and the Tabor Opera House. He also built the Tabor Grand Opera House in Denver. And he gave away hundreds of thousands of dollars to practically anyone who asked for money.

But all was not roses and sunshine for H.A.W. Tabor. His popularity took a hit when the miners went on strike because mine owners had cut their daily wages; Tabor broke the strike by calling in the state militia. Nor did things go well at home after he began accumulating enormous wealth.

Augusta Tabor had labored side by side with her husband during the many lean years. Hardworking and thrifty, she didn't want the comforts and pleasures that H.A.W.'s wealth brought. She felt the money was undeserved and was causing her husband to be excessive in his eating and drinking. Augusta withdrew and became hostile. H.A.W. was, of course, enjoying life immensely and became increasingly irritated with his wife's unbending attitude.

Then he met Elizabeth Bondouell McCourt Doe, who had left an unhappy marriage in Central City and come to Leadville to snag Colorado's richest man. She was successful. Nicknamed "Baby" because of her small stature, the young, blond, vivacious, and lovable Baby Doe agreed to be his mistress, and also agreed to accept the jewels, clothes and other luxuries that H.A.W. wanted his woman to have.

H.A.W. then divorced Augusta and married Baby Doe—twice. The first took place secretly in St. Louis, the second in Washington, D.C. during his 30-day stint as U.S. Senator. President Chester A. Arthur was the guest of honor.

Back in Leadville, and in their new Denver mansion, H.A.W. and Baby Doe had two daughters and enjoyed their extravagances to the hilt...until silver was replaced by gold-backed paper money in 1893. With his silver mining investments no longer paying, and with debts in the millions because he had overspent, H.A.W. had to sell the two opera houses, the block of buildings he had constructed in Denver, his mansion and, finally, Baby Doe's jewels and other valuables.

Nearly destitute and without offers of help from H.A.W.'s wealthy former friends, the Tabors barely got by until one friend did arrange his appointment as Denver postmaster in January of 1898. H.A.W. died a year later, saying to Baby Doe, "Whatever happens, hold on to the Matchless. It will give you back all that I have lost."

Still in her prime when her 65-year-old husband lost his fortune, 33-year-old Baby Doe surprised everyone by standing by him until his death. After three years of trying to make ends meet in Denver, she took her daughters back to Leadville and lived a pauper's life in an abandoned tool house at the Matchless mine where she died in 1935.

How's that for a riches-to-rags tale and a bizarre love story? Sometimes, truth *is* stranger than fiction.

As we leave Leadville, we think it's appropriate to mention that while gold and silver mining enriched the country and some of its people, there has also been a price to pay. Environmentally, we saw it in the rock piles of Breckenridge, and we can see it in the slag heaps and mine tailings here and in the Cripple Creek-Victor area.

People have paid a price as well. Many came optimistically to the gold country only to leave empty-handed and disillusioned. Some like H.A.W. Tabor did well but lost it all and ended up worse off than when they came. And many underground miners suffered death in their twenties and thirties from silicosis, caused by inhalation of rock dust which became lodged in their lungs.

By the way, Leadville didn't die in the silver crash of 1893. It has had periodic resurgences: in the 1890's when rich veins of gold and iron were discovered, and during the first half of the twentieth century with molybdenum mining and Camp Hale nearby. What's molybdenum, you ask? It's a graphite-like substance that's used to harden steel and iron and makes them more corrosion-resistant.

The Upper Arkansas Valley

Now, let's continue our drive south on the Colorado Scenic and Historic Byway.

The first time we traveled from Leadville to Buena Vista, we thought that this was just another beautiful drive, albeit through a broad, semiarid mountain valley studded by sage, juniper, piñon pine, scrub oak, rabbitbrush and even some cacti. Since then, we've learned some interesting things that should enhance your appreciation of what you're going to see. For more information on this geographic area, we highly recommend Virginia McConnell Simmons' book, *The Upper Arkansas: A Mountain River Valley.*

We've already pointed out the Sawatch Range, which will be on our right during the remainder of this afternoon's drive. The Continental Divide runs through this range. You would be correct in assuming that these mountains were uplifted about 65 million years ago, along with those in Rocky Mountain National Park. But what's different here is that the Sawatch peaks were uplifted higher than anywhere else in Colorado. The "fourteener" mountains in the range, from north to south, are the previously-mentioned Massive and Elbert (second highest and highest), La Plata (fifth highest), Oxford, Harvard (third highest), Columbia, Yale, Princeton, Antero, Tabeguache, and Shavano.

Interestingly, geologists tell us that the Sawatch Range was once the western side of a single uplift that also encompassed the Mosquito Range on our left. The Upper Arkansas Valley was created when the central portion of that uplift subsided and was filled-in with hundreds of feet of deposits from mountain streams. What that means is, we'll be driving *in* the central core of the original uplift between the Sawatch and Mosquito Ranges.

No, the valley was not glaciated. But there is plenty of evidence that the canyons in the Sawatch Mountains were. In fact, if you look closely, you'll notice some of that evidence in the form of massive runoff deposits called alluvial fans, which form a skirt along the base of the Sawatch Range.

What's that? You've heard that there were dinosaurs in this part of the country and you're wondering if they frequented this valley? The answer is yes, and no. Yes, dinosaur bones have been found in the area...six miles north of Cañon City to be exact. But, no, technically they didn't come into this valley, because it didn't exist yet. The Age of Reptiles predated the present Rocky Mountains by many millions of years.

As for the Arkansas River itself, you already know that its headwaters are near Tennessee Pass. And you'll correctly assume that most of the river's water comes from snow and rain runoff from the Sawatch and Mosquito Ranges. That water ends up in the Gulf of

Mexico, having traveled south and eastward across the plains to the state of Arkansas and the Mississippi River.

This river was the route used by white men when they first entered the Upper Arkansas Valley. But not too many came before the gold rush in 1859. The area was visited by the French, Spanish and Mexicans in the 1700's, but not by Americans until after the Louisiana Purchase. In 1806 and 1807, Zebulon Pike's exploration route into Colorado followed the Arkansas River nearly to its headwaters, and in 1819 Stephen Long's expedition got as far as the Royal Gorge, which we'll visit tomorrow. In 1845, John Fremont's second expedition traveled through the valley on its way to California—as did some forty-niners from the southern United States when gold was discovered in the Far West four years later.

The Ute and Arapaho Indians had been in the area for a long time, of course. Many of the mountain passes were well-worn Indian trails, later discovered by mountain men who came in the 1820's and 30's to trap beaver in all the canyons along the Arkansas. Among them were Thomas Fitzpatrick, Jim Beckwourth and Kit Carson. What the trappers learned about the canyons and Indian trails over the mountains would become very useful to gold seekers later on.

Gold was first discovered in the Upper Arkansas Valley in 1859 near the town of Granite and then in many canyons and gulches all along the Sawatch Range. We'll visit one of those canyons tomorrow—Chalk Creek Canyon, southwest of Buena Vista—to see first hand what it was like to live in a remote mountain mining town more than 100 years ago. Gold and silver were also mined in pockets along the Mosquito Range.

As we drive farther south into the valley, you'll become aware of the area's second-largest industry after mining: agriculture. Flour millers showed up first, to help feed the hungry miners, especially the throng in Leadville. Next came the hay and oat farmers whose products were needed, along with pastureland, to feed the thousands of horses and mules which pulled ore and supply wagons, stagecoaches and other conveyances of the day. Then came cattle and dairy ranchers, potato farmers and vegetable gardeners, with lettuce being king in the Buena Vista area from 1920 to 1945.

Buena Vista; if you're like us, you'll want to pronounce the name correctly. The locals don't say "Bway-na Vista," as in the Spanish version. They say "Byou-na Vista." (When in Rome, do as the Romans do.)

As you'll see, Buena Vista hasn't changed much since the beginning of the last century. As an overnight stopping place, we think it provides a comfortable contrast with the busier towns on our tour. Once a supply center for the mines and an important stop along three railroads, today it's a laid back ranching town whose primary businesses are whitewater river rafting and the State of Colorado's Buena Vista Correctional Facility.

The town's main attribute is a fantastic view of the Collegiate Peaks in the Sawatch Range: Mounts Oxford, Harvard, Columbia, Yale and Princeton. The reason the Sawatch Range looks so dramatic from 7,944-foot-high Buena Vista is that the mountains rise more than 6,000 feet—well over a mile—above the valley floor. The symmetrical mountain on the left with the Hortense Mine wagon road crossing above timberline is Mount Princeton. On the lower left side of Mt. Princeton, you'll see a white slash which is the opening of Chalk Creek Canyon, where we'll be heading tomorrow morning.

It's Dinnertime!

- **Buffalo Bar & Grill**, American/buffalo, casual, 710 N. Hwy 24, 719-395-6472, no website, $$-$$$.
- **Casa del Sol**, 333 N. Hwy 24, 719-395-8810. Excellent cuisine from the Sonora, Jalisco, Guerrero and Chihuahua regions of Mexico, plus steaks and scampi. Bright and colorful. Casa del Sol is on Bill's personal list of ten best Mexican restaurants in the United States, no website, $-$$.
- **Cyrano's Restaurant & Lounge,** cross-cultural menu, casual elegance, 605 S. Hwy 24, Buena Vista, 719-395-2400, *www.cyranosrestaurant.com*, $$-$$$.
- **Jan's Restaurant**, American, casual, 304 S. Hwy 24, Buena Vista, 719-395-6940, no website, $$.
- **The Missing Spoon**, cuisine and ambiance are eclectic, 314 Charles St., 719-395-0303, *www.missingspoon.com*, $$.

Ginnodo-recommended B&Bs/Resort

- **The Adobe Inn**, 303 N. Hwy 24, Buena Vista, CO 81211, 719-395-6340, 888-343-6340, *www.bbonline.com/co/adobe*, no email address, $$.
- **The Inn at Buena Vista,** 832 S. Gunnison Ave., Buena Vista 81211, 719-395-9293, 877-Inn-ATBV, *www.innatbuenavista.com, stay@innatbuenavista.com,* $$.

- **Las Manos Bed & Breakfast,** 32889 CR 371, Buena Vista 81211, 719-395-4567, *www.lasmanosbandb.com*, email from website, $$.
- **Liar's Lodge**, 30000 CR 371, Buena Vista, CO 81211, 719-395-3444, 888-542-7756, *www.liarslodge.com*, email from website, some French, Spanish, $$.
- **Mount Princeton Hot Springs Resort**, 15870 County Rd. 162, Nathrop, CO 81236, 719-395-2447, 888-395-7799, fax 719-395-6249, *www.mtprinceton.com, info@mtprinceton.com,* $-$$.
- **Sawatch Vistas B&B**, (summers only) 27627 Rancho Sawatch, Buena Vista, CO 81211, 719-395-9199, 866-395-9199, *www.sawatchbedandbreakfast.com*, *info@sawatchbedandbreakfast .com,* $$.
- **Streamside B&B**, 18820 County Road 162, Nathrop, CO 81236, 719-395-2553, *www.southwesterninns.com/strmside.htm*, *streamside@amigo.net*, $.
- **More B&Bs at** *www.innsofcolorado.org*, and *www.colorado-bnb.com.*

AAA- or Mobil-recommended Motels/Hotels

- **Alpine Lodge**, 12845 Hwy 24 & 285, Buena Vista 81211, 888-322-4224, 719-395-2415, fax 719-395-3415, *www.vtinet.com/alpine*, email from website, $.
- **Best Western Vista Inn**, P.O. Box 1101, 733 N. US 24, Buena Vista 81211, 719-395-8009, 800-809-3495, Fax: 719-395-6025, *www.bwvistainn.com*, email from website, $$.
- **Super 8 Motel**, 530 N. US 24, Buena Vista 81211, 719-395-8888, 888-605-8034, fax: 719-395-4090, *www.super8bv.com*, email from website, $-$$.

Woodall's-recommended RV Parks & Campgrounds

- **Arkansas River Rim Campgrounds & RV Park:** Buena Vista; from jct Hwy 306/US 24 go 4-1/2 mi N on US 24; 719-395-8883, *www.arkriverrim.com, rvpark@arkriverrim.com.*
- **Arrowhead Point Camping Resort:** Buena Vista; from jct 285 & US 24, go 98 miles north on US 24; 719-395-2323, 800-888-7320 *www.arrowheadpointresort.com.*
- **Buena Vista-KOA:** Buena Vista; from jct US 24/US 285, go 1-1/4 mi E on US 24/285, then 1/4 mi N on CR 303; 719-395-8318, 800-562-2672, *www.buenavistakoa.com, info@buenavistakoa.com.*

- **Chalk Creek Campground and RV Park:** Nathrop; from jct US 285 and US 24, go 5 miles S. on US 285; 888-395-8830, *www.chalkcreek-campground.com*, *chalkcreek@mccoymail.net.*
- **Mt. Princeton RV Park & Cabins:** Buena Vista; from stop light at north edge of Buena Vista, go 1 mi N on US 24 then 500 feet E on CR 383; 719-395-6206, 888-995-6206, *www.mtprincetonrvpark .com.*
- **Snowy Peaks RV & Mobile Park:** Buena Vista; from jct US 24 and 285, go 1-1/2 mi N on US 24; 719-395-8481, 800-954-8481, *www.snowypeaksrvpark.com.*

Day Five: Five Canyons Along the Arkansas

Today, instead of just driving by all this wonderful scenery, we're going to get up close and personal with some of it. This morning, we'll make a foray into the Sawatch Range where we'll enjoy nature's beauty and serenity in Chalk Creek Canyon, take a look at Colorado's best-preserved ghost town, and hike along the Colorado Trail. This afternoon, we'll drive through spectacular Arkansas River Canyon, experience the heights and depths of the Royal Gorge, and explore our way up Phantom Canyon to Cripple Creek...if you're game.

Speaking of being game...If you're on an extended tour and have a taste for adventure, you may want to try whitewater rafting on the Arkansas River. (See the photograph at the beginning of this book.) This is the best place in Colorado to experience the sport; some 300,000 rafters and kayakers come here every year, mid-May through early September. For that reason, *advance reservations are usually necessary*. You have a choice of fairly calm water starting about 12 miles north of Salida, or you can experience rougher water both north and south of Buena Vista. The half-day, 10-mile, Class III-IV Brown's Canyon trip is the most popular, at about $45-50 per person. There are more than 60 state-licensed outfitters running the Arkansas River, so ask your innkeeper to recommend one. Those in the Buena Vista area which have been recommended to us are:

- **American Adventure Expeditions**, located in Johnson Village; P.O. Box 1549, 12844 E. US 24/285, Buena Vista, CO 81211; 719-395-2409, 800-288-0675, *www.americanadventure.com, raftinginfo @americanadventure.com.*
- **Dvorak's Kayak & Rafting Expeditions**, 17921 US 285, Nathrop, CO 81236; 719-539-6851, 800-824-3795, *www.dvorakexpeditions .com, info@dvorakexpeditions.com.*
- **Noah's Ark**, P.O. Box 850, Buena Vista, CO 81211; 719-395-2158, *www.noahsark.com.*
- **Wilderness Aware**, departs from Johnson Village, P.O. Box 1550, Buena Vista, CO 81211; 800-462-7238 or 719-395-2112, *www. inaraft.com, rapids@inaraft.com.* (We used this outfit; they did an excellent job.)

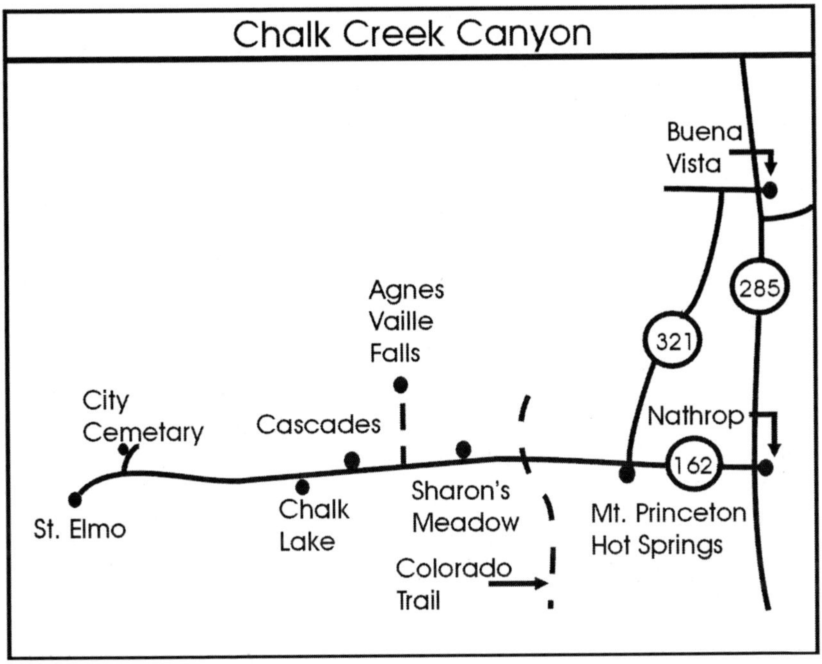

Chalk Creek Canyon and St. Elmo

You should know, before we begin this drive, that there are no services or public bathrooms, except for those at Mt. Princeton Hot Springs Resort.

From the traffic light in Buena Vista, let's head west on Main Street one-half mile to County Road 321/Rodeo St. where we'll turn left, drive 8 miles across the mesa to County Road 162 and then turn right toward the Continental Divide. You'll see Mount Princeton Hot Springs Resort at the junction of CR 321 and CR 162. It's here that we suggest you take a mileage reading, so we can better guide you.

As we enter Chalk Creek Canyon between Mt. Princeton on your right and Mt. Antero on your left, you may be interested to learn a couple of things. The first is that this is one of several places in the Upper Arkansas River Valley where geothermal springs bubble up from deep in the earth. The springs have provided soothing baths for human beings since they were first discovered by Native Americans many years before white men came. (If you are on an extended tour, Mount Princeton Hot Springs Resort is a good place to experience swimming or soaking in clean, clear, odor-free hot mineral water).

The other thing is related to the first: the white cliffs on your right have been made "chalky" by the leaching of hot springs upward through fissures in the rocks. The powdery white rock is called kaolinite. As you'll see, the cliffs add an element of beauty to the canyon that will help you remember this drive for a very long time. (See the photograph at the beginning of this book.)

To get maximum enjoyment from this 10-mile drive, we'd like to suggest that you get out of the car four or five times before reaching St. Elmo in order to better take in the serenity of this canyon and the San Isabel National Forest. Four spots in particular provide especially nice viewing.

First is Sharon's Meadow, a wildlife viewing area, three miles from the CR 321/162 junction, on the right. Our last time at Sharon's Meadow, we saw six bighorn sheep feeding, about 20 feet from the road. The reader board provides interesting information on the flora and fauna of the area.

Second is Agnes Vaille Falls, one mile farther, also on the right. We recommend the one-half mile hike to the falls, not to see something spectacular (it's not), but, as we suggested earlier, to "get up close and personal" with the scenery. You'll have another chance to hike, along the Colorado Trail, in a little while.

Third, a mile later, you'll come to the Cascades, which is also worth a close-up look if the water is flowing well.

Lastly, one mile past the Cascades, you'll come upon Chalk Lake, on your left. Here, you'll see a beaver hut and a beaver dam holding water back from the road.

Have you been noticing the pleasant vistas along Chalk Creek and the beautiful aspen groves on the left? Harking back to our tutorial on trees while in Rocky Mountain National Park, you'll remember that the presence of aspens means we're in the montane life zone, somewhere between 7,000 and 9,500 feet in elevation.

When you arrive in St. Elmo (10,012 feet), we suggest that you walk to the other end of town, slowly taking it all in, then return to our narrative.

* * * * *

OK, you're back. Here's the scoop on St. Elmo.

Would you believe that some 1,000 people lived here during the 1880's and 1890's? And that the Denver, South Park and Pacific

Railway came up Chalk Creek Canyon to St. Elmo? (Yes, that was the old railroad roadbed you were driving on.)

Originally called Forest City, St. Elmo was a junction point for wagons and stagecoaches heading up the North Fork of Chalk Creek and over the Continental Divide at Tincup Pass (to your right and up the mountain). When the railroad completed the Alpine Tunnel through the Divide above town in 1882, St. Elmo became the trade and transportation center for the mines in this area. The tunnel was in use intermittently until 1910. The railroad continued operations along Chalk Creek and its South Fork (to your left) until 1926, particularly in support of the Mary Murphy Mine, which was the most famous and productive silver mine in the area.

In addition to the usual services, such as restaurants, saloons, livery stable, blacksmith, druggist and hardware store, St. Elmo had five hotels, a sawmill, a hydroelectric power plant and four ore-crushing stamp mills.

Knowing that, you may be able to imagine what this town was like in its heyday...miners, travelers and merchants carrying on their business in the various establishments...wagons, stagecoaches and horses moving about the main street...the train chugging and whistling toward town...the stamp mills thudding in the distance...all nearly drowning out the clang of the blacksmith's hammer on his anvil. This may be a "ghost town," but it was once a good-sized, living, breathing business center and community, typical of others throughout these mountains.

What makes it atypical is that so much of St. Elmo still stands. Elsewhere, fires, scavengers, vandals, time and the elements have reduced most of the old mining camps to a few log cabins and miscellaneous structures. St. Elmo, however, is now protected by preservationists, its residents, and its status as a national historic district—so future generations can see and enjoy the real thing.

Mostly, we have Annabelle Stark (who used her shotgun to run off intruders who were a danger to her beloved town) to thank for the preservation of St. Elmo. Annabelle and her brother, Tony, ran the Stark Brothers General Store, and Home Comfort Hotel, on the second floor, until the 1950's. (See the photograph at the beginning of this book.)

On a personal note, Bill has a fond memory of riding into St. Elmo on horseback about 11:30 on a clear, crisp late-summer night in 1955 with two other wranglers from nearby Frontier Ranch. The full moon was shining on the false-fronted buildings. There were no sounds except for the clip-clop of the horses' hooves and creaking of our leather saddles. As we passed Stark Brothers, we could see a light in the back of the store and knew that Annabelle and Tony were still awake. Fifteen minutes later, we were in our sleeping bags enjoying the gurgling of Chalk Creek and savoring the historic reverie that St. Elmo had cast upon us.

While you're still on the western side of town, take a few minutes to explore the creek. We found a walk along its banks to be very lovely and relaxing.

There is one other thing we'd like you to see before we leave the area: St. Elmo City Cemetery. To get there, head back down CR 162 about a quarter mile, turn left at the Iron City sign and drive 0.6 mile. This cemetery-in-the-woods is neat, peaceful and has many gravesites dating from the 1880s and 1890s. Some of them are graves of children, individually fenced to protect them from animals.

OK, let's retrace our drive east toward the Mt. Princeton Hot Springs Resort, where we'll have lunch. If you get close to the resort at about 11 am, as we anticipate, you'll have plenty of time for a hike on the Colorado Trail. You'll find the trail about a mile and a half past Agnes Vaille Falls. There's a large parking pullout on the left, where you'll see a National Forest information board. Across the road from the pullout and down the driveway, you'll find a smaller parking area where we recommend you begin your hike.

Here's what we suggest about timing: Hike as long as you wish, but keep in mind that the Mount Princeton Hot Springs Resort restaurant serves lunch from 11 am to 2 pm. To get the most out of our afternoon activities, we should be heading toward the Royal Gorge by about 1:30 pm.

As we hike southward, you'll be interested to know that the Colorado Trail is 469 miles long and stretches from Denver in the northeast quadrant of the state to Durango in the southwest.

Mt. Antero will be on our right as we walk. Interestingly, there's a well-known gem field near the summit of this mountain where people collect gem-quality minerals such as blue and green aquamarines, topaz, smoky quartz and rock crystal. There are also gem fields on nearby Mt. White and on Ruby Mountain across the valley. By the way, Mt. Antero is one of the major peaks in the southern part of the Sawatch Range that are named for Ute Indians: Antero, Shavano and Ouray were chiefs; Chipeta was Chief Ouray's wife and Pahlone was his son; and Tabequache was the name of the Ute band that frequented this area.

While at Mount Princeton Hot Springs Resort for lunch, we thought you'd like to know that this was the site of the four-story Antero Hotel, which was operational for most of the period between 1917 and 1950, when it was torn down. A million board feet of its lumber was shipped to Texas to be used in new home construction. Today, some 90,000 visitors come here each year to swim and soak in the resort's three swimming pools and in the small pools in Chalk Creek. If you want to *really* get up close and personal with the landscape, try a relaxing soak in the Chalk Creek hot spring pools.

Buena Vista to Cripple Creek

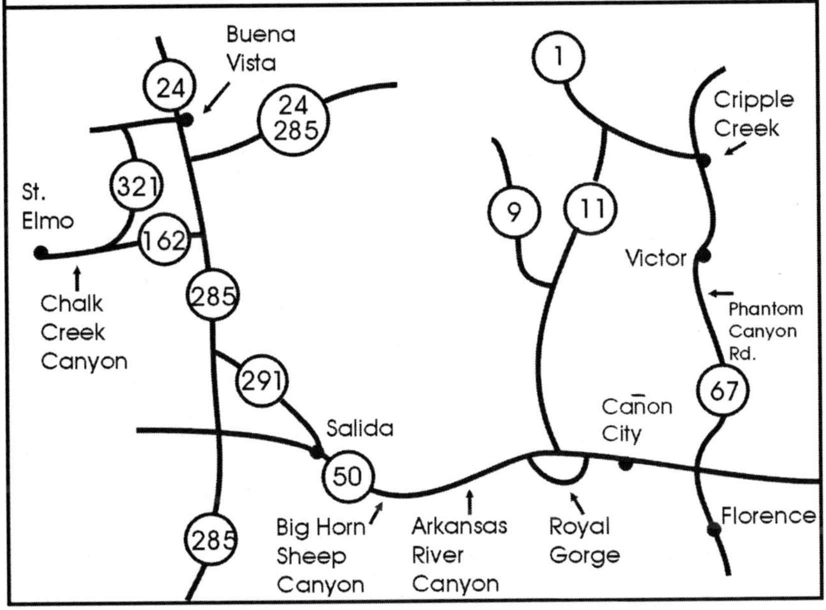

The Arkansas River Canyon

From Mount Princeton Hot Springs Resort, drive east on CR 162 (don't turn onto CR 270) five miles to its intersection with US 285 at Nathrop. Then turn right, drive eight miles, and turn left onto Colorado 291 toward Salida. The mountain range that you see off to your right at this point is the Sangre de Cristo.

As you approach Salida, you'll see a tall, red smokestack on your right standing all by itself and will wonder what it is, as we did our first time through here. It's what's left of Smeltertown, a complex of buildings and smokestacks employing 500 people and operated by the Ohio and Colorado Smelting and Refining Company between 1901 and 1919. This smokestack was built to its unusual height of 364 feet (36 stories!) in an attempt to project noxious smoke higher into the atmosphere. Smeltertown used its furnaces to separate gold, silver and other minerals from ores mined throughout the Upper Arkansas River Valley.

When you arrive in Salida, continue on Colorado 291 until it intersects with US 50, then turn east toward Cañon City. Soon, you'll enter Bighorn Sheep Canyon, then a long valley, followed by the Arkansas River Canyon. You'll see the tracks and tunnels of the Denver and Rio Grande Western Railroad paralleling the river and road on your left, and if you're lucky as we were, a train will accompany you part of the way, adding to the excitement of the drive.

The Arkansas River Canyon was a very pleasant surprise to us the first time we came through here. Having no previous knowledge of it, we kept saying, "What an adventure!" Looking at the map, we had anticipated a colorless, dry, wasteland. Dry it may be, except, of course, for the river, but it certainly is not colorless, and its beauty wasn't wasted on us.

Some 20 miles long, the canyon is a very big part of the river's 1,400-foot drop from Salida's 7,036-foot elevation to 5,635 feet at the Royal Gorge. But, to us, on a sunny day, the canyon's greatest feature was its red sandstone hills, accented by light green sage and a beautiful blue sky. It reminded us of the red rock country in Sedona, Arizona. Celia called the Arkansas River Canyon "awesome." Bill still thinks of this drive as a long, delicious slide through butterscotch pudding (his favorite).

The Royal Gorge Suspension Bridge

Soon after you leave the canyon, you'll have a decision to make when you see a highway sign on the right that reads, "Royal Gorge, 2-1/2 Miles." That is: "to cross, or not to cross the bridge." Ignore this sign if you want to drive across the Royal Gorge Bridge. Look for the Parkdale sign and turn right onto Fremont County Road 3. *FCR 3 is open Memorial Day/late May through Labor Day/early September. If you are traveling before or after those dates, simply continue on US 50 to the main entrance to the bridge.*

What do we recommend? If you're driving an RV that's larger than a van or small camper, you won't be permitted on the bridge. If you've been comfortable with the driving on this trip thus far, and have no great fear of heights, by all means drive across the bridge. It's a unique and thrilling experience, albeit unsettling to the driver. In addition to that, Fremont County Road 3 is unique and well worth seeing: a six and one-half mile, otherworldly country lane through hilly meadows studded with low-growing trees and having no signs of civilization.

At the toll booth, you'll be charged $23 per person to cross the bridge, but this fee also includes entrance to the incline railway, aerial tramway, and access to the rest of Royal Gorge Park, which is a complex of rides, shows and gift shops. (Buy one admission ticket at full price and get the second ½ off.)

The park is open daily: 10 am to 4, 5, 6 or 7 pm (depending on the time of year), P.O. Box 549, Cañon City, CO 81215, 719-275-7507, 888-333-5597; *www.royalgorgebridge.com.*

All right now, take a deep breath and drive off boldly across the bridge! Since you won't have any interest in what we have to say for the next few minutes, just put down the book and enjoy this sensational experience.

* * * * *

Hello, again. There are two other things we'd like to suggest that you do here. The first is to walk (crawl?) out onto the bridge and look at the canyon from a height of 1,053 feet; that's about 100 stories. Even if you've been to the Grand Canyon in Arizona, the view should give you a thrill. This suspension bridge, the highest in the world, was built as a tourist attraction and has been both attracting and thrilling tourists ever since. (See the photograph at the beginning of this book.)

Our second recommendation is to take the five-minute ride on the world's steepest incline railway to the canyon floor. There's an aerial tram that crosses the chasm, but we think the greater experience is to go down next to the river and railroad tracks and look up the steep canyon walls to that ribbon of a bridge high above. Don't you wonder at the challenges that were faced by the railroad company and the bridge builders as they laid tracks through the canyon in 1880, and spanned the gorge in 1929?

Now, we're going to suggest that you look at the clock, because the drive we have ahead of us through Phantom Canyon could take up to 2-1/2 hours. We strongly recommend that you complete it before dark and that will probably mean spending less time in Royal Gorge Park than you might like.

There is an alternative route you can take that will give you a little more time at the park. You may prefer that 45-mile alternate route, with its hard pavement and easier terrain, to the Phantom Canyon route that is dirt and gravel most of its 31 miles, somewhat steeper, and more twisty-turny. If you're driving a motor home or pulling a trailer, you'll have to use the alternate route, because they're prohibited in narrow Phantom Canyon. If it has rained or snowed, or if either is threatening, we also suggest that you use the alternate route; Phantom Canyon is likely to be slippery and difficult to navigate.

In both cases, you'll exit the east side of the park and drive four miles to US 50. For the alternate route, turn left on US 50 and drive 1-1/2 miles to Colorado 9. Then, turn right and travel nine miles north to High Park Road where you'll turn right at the Cripple Creek directional sign. Now, you'll be on Fremont County Road 11, which becomes Teller 11 when you enter Teller County. Twenty miles after you leave Colorado 9, you'll come to Cripple Creek/Florissant Road (Teller County Road 1), where you'll turn right and drive eight miles into Cripple Creek.

Phantom Canyon

We prefer the drive up Phantom Canyon, which is a Colorado Scenic and Historic Byway, part of the popular Gold Belt Tour, and more of an adventure. To get there, drive east 15 miles from where you enter US 50. You'll pass through Cañon City and turn left on Fremont County Road 67. (The town of Florence is to the right.) From there it's 31 miles to Victor and another six miles to Cripple Creek.

Yes, if you've been counting, this will be our fifth canyon of the day: Chalk Creek, Bighorn Sheep, Arkansas River, Royal Gorge, and Phantom. *Canyon*, by the way, is defined by Webster's as "a deep narrow valley with steep sides and often with a stream flowing through it."

As with Chalk Creek Canyon, Phantom Canyon was once the route of a narrow gauge railway that served the mines. In this case, the Florence and Cripple Creek Railroad operated here between 1894 and 1912, primarily carrying ores from Cripple Creek and Victor down to the gold processing facilities in Florence. Originally named after Eightmile Creek, which runs through it, the canyon was given its more mysterious name by railroad people as a way of attracting early sightseers.

And, as in Rocky Mountain National Park, we'll experience a pronounced change in life zones as we gently wind upward from about 5,300 feet to Victor's 9,729-foot elevation, crossing 12 bridges and passing through two tunnels as we go. Please drive slowly and take care as you wend your way up the narrow road, remembering that vehicles coming downhill have the right of way, and that you should not stop on curves where you might be hidden from the view of oncoming drivers.

But, by all means, do stop at several wide spots in the road and enjoy this dramatic and beautiful canyon as you ascend toward Cripple Creek.

***

As you drive through Victor, it's important to mention that this town was the other side of the Cripple Creek Mining District's golden coin. That is, most of the gold in the district was mined in or near Victor, while Cripple Creek—six miles away—was the area's financial, political and social center.

If you look uphill and to the right as we drive through town, you'll see Battle Mountain, site of the district's, and America's, greatest gold producers: the Portland, Independence, Ajax and Strong mines. Tomorrow, we'll drive through the goldfields and learn more about the Independence Mine and its owner.

The other fact of interest about Victor is that this was the hometown and early training ground of world-famous radio, movie and television news broadcaster Lowell Thomas. There's a museum at 3rd and Victor filled with Lowell Thomas memorabilia, mining artifacts and historic documents (*www.victorcolorado.com/museum*).

Continue past Victor on CR 67 until you arrive in Cripple Creek.

It's Dinnertime!

- **Bronco Billy's Steakhouse** (in Buffalo Billy's Casino), American, sports-mounted wildlife, Thur-Sun, 233 E. Bennett Ave., 719-689-2142, no website, $$-$$$.
- **Down Under Steak House** (in the Midnight Rose Casino), American food, Australian ambiance, Thur-Sun, 256 E. Bennett Ave., 719-689-0303, no website, $$-$$$$.
- **Maggie's Restaurant** (in the Colorado Grand Casino), American cuisine, late 1880's, 300 E. Bennett Ave., 719-689-3517, no website, $-$$.
- **Stratton Room** (in the Imperial Hotel; our preference), American cuisine, Victorian ambiance, 123 N. Third St., 719-689-7777, no website, $$-$$$.

Ginnodo-recommended Accommodations

- **Cripple Creek Hospitality House & RV Park**, PO Box 957, 600 N. "B" St., Cripple Creek 80813, 719-689-2513, 800-500-2513, fax 719-689-2513, *www.cchospitalityhouse.com,* $-$$.
- **Hotel St. Nicholas**, PO Box 1459, 303 N. Third St., Cripple Creek 80813, 719-689-0856, 888-786-4257, fax 719-689-2877, *www.cripple-creek.co.us/stnick.html*, *akelly600@aol.com*, $.
- **Last Dollar Inn B&B**, PO Box 1199, 315 E. Carr Ave., Cripple Creek 80813, 719-689-9113, 888-429-6700, fax 719-689-0868, *www.cripple-creek.co.us/lastdinn.htm,* *packy578@concentric.net,* $-$$ (we really like this place).
- **More B&Bs at** *www.innsofcolorado.org*, and *www.coloradobnb.com.*

AAA- or Mobil-recommended Motels/Hotels

- **Carr Manor,** PO Box 189, 350 E. Carr Ave., Cripple Creek 80813, 719-689-3709, fax 719-689-2140, *www.carrmanor.com, reservations@carrmanor.com,* $$-$$$.
- **Gold King Mountain Inn,** PO Box 1329, 601 E. Galena Ave., Cripple Creek 80813, 719-689-2600, 800-445-3607, fax 719-689-3426, *www.gkmi.com*, $-$$.

Woodall's-recommended RV Parks & Campgrounds

- **Cripple Creek Hospitality House & RV Park:** from center of town at jct 2nd St & Bennett Ave, go 1/4 mi W on Bennett Ave, then 5 blocks N past school on B St.; 800-500-2513, *www.cchospitalityhouse.com*
- **Eagles Landing RV Park:** Cripple Creek; from center of town at jct 2nd St & Bennett Ave, go S 2 blocks to Warren and turn right; 719-689-2006, *www.cripplecreekrv.com.*
- **KOA-Cripple Creek:** from jct Hwy 67 & Teller 81, go 1/2 mi S on Teller 81 toward Victor; 719-689-3376.
- **Lost Burro Campground:** Cripple Creek; from center of town at jct 2nd St & Bennett Ave, go 1/4 mi W on Bennett Ave, then 200 feet N on B St., then 3-1/2 mi NW on CR 1; 719-689-2345, 877-689-2345, *www.lostburro.com, lostburro@ccvnet.net.*
- **Mueller State Park:** Divide; from Cripple Creek, go 14-1/2 mi N on Hwy 67; 719-687-2366, *http://parks.state.co.us/parks/mueller.*

Day Six: The World's Greatest Gold Camp

Guaranteed to be another interesting day, here's what we've got in store for you: First, we'll set the stage with the story of Bob Womack, the cowboy who wanted only satisfaction and recognition—not wealth—from his discovery of Cripple Creek's goldfields. Next, we'll descend 1,000 feet into the Mollie Kathleen Mine to see a genuine vein of gold and learn how hard rock miners made their living. That will be followed by a drive through the goldfields, a visit to Cripple Creek's excellent museum, and a view of the city that should help you appreciate what a vibrant place this was at the turn of the 20th century.

After lunch, you'll get to gamble some, then we'll examine some interesting plant and animal fossils, take a nature walk, and visit a pioneer woman's 1878 homestead near Florissant. After that, we'll head for our evening meal and night's lodging in the Colorado Springs area.

Two alternative activities are: visit a classy brothel called The Old Homestead, or take a hike and enjoy the scenery at Mueller State Park. You'll find brochures for these attractions in the museum, in some stores and at the Welcome Center in front of the museum.

During your travels today, be on the lookout for the donkeys that roam freely; some are descendants of animals that pulled ore carts in the mines more than a hundred years ago. They're owned and maintained by a local business boosters club.

World's Most Generous Prospector

Here's a conundrum, a mystery, for you to think about: Why would someone *not* want to cash in on the riches of a gold or silver mine that he discovered? One of H.A.W. Tabor's German shoemaker partners was like that; he chose to sell out cheaply and leave Leadville for the simple life. "Crazy Bob" Womack was also like that; he begged people to come and take advantage of his find, then gave away what little he personally earned from it.

Womack was a fun-loving cowboy who liked to prospect for gold. After learning that the area where his family lived was the crater of an extinct volcano, and that gold and silver were often found in such a site, he persisted in his search for 14 years. But when he did find a rich deposit of gold in October of 1890, no one would believe him. Locally, he had a reputation for heavy drinking and hi-jinx. Folks in Colorado

Springs didn't believe him because of a recent hoax in which a couple of hustlers "salted" a nearby mine with high-grade ore in order to sell it.

Frustrated, Womack told everyone who would listen and still found no one interested—until a dentist, a German count, and a prospector-turned-carpenter looked a little more closely. Of the three, the carpenter, Winfield Scott Stratton, was the most fortunate. He reluctantly made the 30-mile trek from Colorado Springs to Cripple Creek in July of 1892, saw that Womack's story was accurate, staked a claim on the Independence Mine, became the first of Cripple Creek's 30 millionaires, and went on to own about one-third of the district. Stratton sold the Independence to an English corporation for $11 million, which is more than $100 million in today's dollars.

Here's an interesting aside: Do you remember our telling you about H.A.W. Tabor losing his fortune in Leadville and being appointed to the Denver postmaster position? Well, it was Winfield Scott Stratton who arranged the appointment and who gave Tabor survival money when he hit bottom.

And here is a second side-story: Another of the 30 Cripple Creek millionaires, a pharmacist, was even luckier than Stratton. He didn't need Womack's help. Not knowing where to start, he threw his hat into the air and dug where it landed, discovering a rich vein of gold.

For his part, Bob Womack was for a while a local hero for having discovered half a dozen famous mines and making a lot of people wealthy. He reportedly enjoyed the notoriety and vindication over many bottles of bourbon. But he sold his initial claim without working it and gave away the money. The mine eventually produced $5 million in gold. In one of the great ironies of all time, the discoverer of the World's Greatest Gold Camp died as a forgotten and destitute stroke victim.

By the way, are you wondering where the name "Cripple Creek" came from? Some years before Bob Womack made his discovery, a neighboring rancher first uttered the words when one of his calves broke a leg jumping a local stream: "Well boys, this sure is some cripple creek!" Womack put the name in general circulation when he responded to folks in Colorado Springs who asked where he'd made his discovery: "Why, on Cripple Creek!"

The Mollie Kathleen Mine

OK, let's take that gold mine tour.

But, first, you may want to stop for a few minutes in front of the Cripple Creek District Museum, at the east end of Bennett St., to learn what the Welcome Center has to offer; 1-877-858-GOLD, *www.cripple-creek.co.us*.

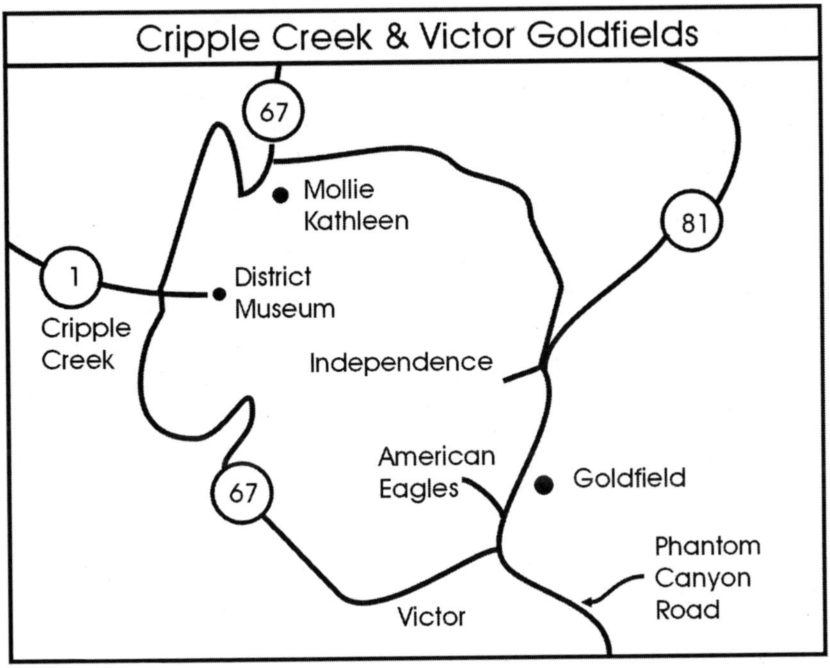

Now, drive northeast from town on Colorado 67, 0.9 mile, where you'll find the Mollie Kathleen Mine, on your right, overlooking Cripple Creek. The mine is open for hour-long tours 9 am to 5 pm, seven days a week, April through October. Tours are sometimes available off-season; call ahead. The telephone number, in case you want the comfort of a reservation, is 719-689-2466 or 888-291-5689; *www.goldminetours.com, molliegold@rmi.net.*

This is a genuine hard rock mine that was in operation from 1892 until 1961. You'll descend 1,000 feet through solid granite—no cave-ins in this mine—which means that you'll be 600 feet below the level of Cripple Creek. And your tour guide may be a genuine miner. There's an authenticity here that helps the visitor comprehend what underground hard rock mining is all about.

That feeling of authenticity begins when you and six other people squeeze into the miners cage, referred to as a "skip," and begin your two-minute descent. You'll be provided with a jacket, so won't mind the mine's cool temperature as you take the 35- to 40-minute tour.

(Speaking of "skip," Celia says she wouldn't have skipped this experience for the world.)

What you'll see is an underground tunnel with a real gold vein overhead, mining equipment, and a display of gold in its various forms. What you'll learn, among other things, is how the miners searched for and followed gold along tunnels called "drifts" and "crosscuts," and that this is the only place in the world where there's gold in solid granite. (When the volcano erupted, cracks were opened in the rock, into which gold was forced.) Only 20 percent of the available gold has been taken out of the Mollie Kathleen. Yes, hard rock miners insist that 80 percent of the area's precious metal is still in the ground, just waiting for the price of gold to climb to the point where mining becomes economical again.

Before we head off on this next part of the drive, you may want to consider an alternative: The Cripple Creek & Victor Narrow Gauge Railroad, which departs from the Cripple Creek District Museum every 45 minutes and takes folks on a narrated, albeit more limited, tour. (It does not go all the way to Victor.)

This is an active mining area. It's important that you stay away from the mines and dumps as they can be unstable and dangerous, and all are on private property. They are fenced off for your safety.

A Goldfields Drive

So, with that caution in mind, let's set your vehicle's trip odometer to 0. We want you to have exact mileage readings for stopping points on this drive. Then, turn immediately to the right as you exit the mine's parking lot and enter the gravel road that runs through the heart of the goldfields. Proceed only about 0.1 mile.

Below you stretches Poverty Gulch, site of the first gold discovery by "Crazy Bob" Womack. Mine headframes visible from this point, from left to right, include: the Colorado King, halfway up the hill and silhouetted against the sky, the Anchoria Leland, which produced as much as $60,000 in gold per month, below it the C.O.D. Mine, and below that the Proper. Just to the left of the Mollie Kathleen is the Gold King, another famous producer. The C.O.D. Mine started Spencer Penrose, who later built the famous Broadmoor Hotel in Colorado Springs, on the road to wealth.

By the way, a "headframe" is the structure that held the hoist that was used to lower and raise the miners and their equipment.

Proceed up the hill an additional 0.7-mile to the intersection. This area is known as Hoosier Pass (elevation 10,300 ft). The Hoosier Mine headframe lies to the east (or your left). To the right of the headframe is the western face of Pikes Peak (elevation 14,108 ft.), with the automobile road to the summit faintly visible.

Next, continue another 1.4 mile. The three red buildings on your left are all that remain of the town of Midway. The one on the right was the Midway Saloon, a favorite watering hole for miners waiting for the next trolley to or from work.

Now, continue 1.0 mile to the end of this road and turn right at the intersection onto CR 831, just before the paved road. After 0.5 mile, you'll come upon the Vindicator Mine. You may want to walk around the Vindicator to get the feel for aboveground workings and mine buildings.

Just past the Vindicator, you'll come to a turnaround. A short way up the hill, behind the rocks that block the roadway, was the town of Independence, which had a population of 1,500. It was the Independence Railroad Station that Harry Orchard dynamited for the Western Federation of Miners, killing 13 men as they waited for a train during the District's labor wars.

Then, return to the intersection with the paved road, CR 81, and take an odometer reading. We don't want you to miss the turnoff to American Eagles. About a mile down the road, you'll come upon the town of Goldfield, which had a population of 3,500 in 1900. Today it's the third largest community in the District.

When your odometer tells you that you've traveled 1.9 miles, you should be at the right-hand turnoff to the American Eagles Mine. From here, you'll proceed 2.5 miles upward, through a landscape and to a view that you'll remember for quite a while.

Don't be dissuaded by the roughness of the road as you start uphill; it's a lot smoother most of the way to the top.

Last evening, as you drove through Victor, we promised a closer look at Battle Mountain. You'll be passing it—and the Independence (Winfield Scott Stratton's original discovery), Strong, Portland and Ajax mines—as you ascend.

At the top of the drive, you'll want to read the descriptive markers placed near the buildings of the American Eagles Mine, which is the highest underground mine in the District at 10,700 feet and was also once owned by Stratton.

But, even more, you'll want to look at the view...at both the inspirational and the depressing.

About 50 air miles in the distance, you'll see a mountain range, called the Sangre de Cristo (blood of Christ), so named by early Spanish explorers because of the pinkish hue on the snow of the peaks. (You may remember us pointing out the range as we approached Salida.)

The huge open mine pit below is the site of the Cresson Mine. This was one of the most famous mines in the world, because $500,000 in gold was taken from a single chamber...when gold sold for only $20.67 per ounce. (At the time of this book's publication, gold was above $650!) The Cripple Creek & Victor Gold Mining Company is actively mining the Cresson today.

After completing your descent to the bottom of the hill, turn right, and then left 0.1 mile later at the Elk's Club, into Victor's business district. Turn right at the stop sign and you'll be on Colorado 67 heading toward Cripple Creek.

On your right 0.1 mile later, you'll find Victor's City Hall and a rather interesting display on the history of the area. As the second largest city in the District, Victor once had a population of 18,000. Today the population is under 300. Behind the city hall was located the Gold Coin Mine, discovered during excavation for what was to have been the new Victor Hotel in 1893.

Less than a mile farther on, you'll come to a 700-ft. high heap leach, on your right. This is a modern-day method of gold mining in which a low-level cyanide water solution is dripped onto crushed ore to dissolve and recover the valuable mineral. And, yes, the cyanide is kept from getting into the earth and water system by means of rubber bladders under the ore and with sensors to detect leaks.

Finally, proceed to Cripple Creek and turn right on Bennett.

All Was Not As It Appears

When you've finished your drive of the goldfields, walk up the steps of the Cripple Creek District Museum. Now, turn around and take a good look at Cripple Creek National Historic District spread out before you.

It may be difficult to imagine, but at its peak in 1900, Cripple Creek was famous all across America and around the world, and was a thoroughly modern city teeming with people and activity. Some 25,000 people lived in Cripple Creek, 18,000 lived in Victor, and 13,000 more lived in 13 other area towns. That's 56,000 miners, business people, and some of their families, all focused on extracting gold from the ground and from each other.

And there was a lot of gold: more than $18 million was produced during 1900 alone. In total, over the years, the 24-square-mile district's

$600 million in gold production was more than California's and Alaska's combined. That's about $12 billion in today's dollars!

All of this wealth allowed Cripple Creek—even at 9,494 feet elevation—to have the latest conveniences and diversions: electricity, telephones, running water to every lot, four of the finest department stores in the state (special trains carried shoppers from Colorado Springs to Cripple Creek to see the latest fashions from Paris), two modern hospitals, seven drug stores, 49 grocery stores, 20 meat markets, 11 dairies, 14 bakeries, 11 laundries, 11 blacksmith shops, five livery stables, eight newspapers, a stock exchange, two opera houses (one with 800 seats), a vaudeville theater, modern hotels, 16 churches, 19 schools, 73 saloons and an extensive red light district.

Another dynamic of the time that you may have difficulty imagining is that there was a lot of movement throughout the area. Crowds of people gathered in these streets on special occasions. (At the museum, pick up a copy of Leland Feitz's pamphlet, "Cripple Creek! A Quick History," and you'll see that fact for yourself.) People rode in all kinds of conveyances, including the electric trolley system that connected the area's towns and mines until 1920, enabling residents to travel comfortably to and from work, school and shopping. (Remember, this was before the automobile became the common mode of transportation.) And there were three railroads with two depots serving the area, with as many as 58 daily trains carrying gold ore, miners and visitors into and out of the district every day.

So, despite its remote mountain location, the Cripple Creek Mining District was one of the most prosperous and lively population centers in America.

Cripple Creek did have serious labor problems, however, and two fires, four days apart in 1896, which almost totally destroyed the town. That's why you see so many brick buildings; the shop owners and other residents weren't about to have that happen again! By the way, Victor was similarly destroyed in 1899 and was also rebuilt with brick.

A First-class Museum

Please don't think of this as "just another museum in a country town." After what you've already seen and learned about the Cripple Creek Mining District, an hour or two spent here will make the area's history come alive.

There are actually three buildings to this wonderful museum. In the Assay Office you can observe how local ores were tested for mineral content, and examine the interesting geology and mining collections. In the Colorado Trading & Transfer Building, you can see a natural history exhibit, a collection of historic photographs, and a gallery of locally produced art.

We suspect that you'll spend most of your time on the three levels of the main building, examining the depictions of life in Cripple Creek between 1890 and 1910, and the three-dimensional model showing the miles of drifts (hunting for gold) and cross-cuts (following gold) that were carved into solid granite down to 3,200 ft. underground at the Portland Mine. Altogether, the district has 2,500 *miles* of such tunnels! The main building was built in 1895 and served as the depot of the Midland Terminal Railroad until 1949.

The **Cripple Creek District Museum**, is open year-round: June 1-Sept. 30 from 10 am to 5 pm; Oct. 1- May 31 from 10 am to 4 pm; PO Box 1210, Cripple Creek 80813, 719-689-2634, *www.cripple-creek .org*.

So, what's next...a little lunch, some gambling, or a walk up and down Bennett Avenue? We suggest: all three.

For lunch, locals recommend **Maggie's Restaurant** in the Colorado Grand Casino, the **3rd Street Deli** in the Imperial Casino and the **Home Cafe** in Buffalo Billy's Casino. But, be prepared for a lot of hubbub while you eat.

After lunch, take that walk up and down Bennett Ave. and try to imagine what it was like to live and work here around the turn of the last century.

Win or Lose (a Little), It's Fun

We're not gamblers, so we viewed this next activity as novel entertainment. Our objective was to risk no more than $10 and see if we could stretch it for an hour.

Right off, we found a way to increase our nest egg without gambling a cent: We left our car in a lot run by a casino which gave us a $5 voucher redeemable only in their establishment. Free parking, free money; not bad for a couple of vacationing fun-seekers!

So we entered the casino, forked over the voucher and $10 for quarters, and headed for the slot machines near the front door. The latter we did on the advice of Bill's sister, who told him she'd heard from a reputable source that those machines are set so as to pay off more often—with quarters jangling noisily into the trays—in order to draw passing tourists into the casino. (Don't tell anyone at the casino you know this or you'll ruin it for those who follow.)

We have only our one experience to go by, but it worked for us! Exactly one hour later, we walked out of the casino $33.50 richer than when we'd entered—and enjoyed a couple of free soft drinks, besides!

Of course, you needn't try to replicate our experience. Park in a pay lot; use the slot machines in the back corner; branch out to blackjack or poker; lose some money; turn down the free drinks; stay there all afternoon; or skip the casinos altogether—whatever turns you on.

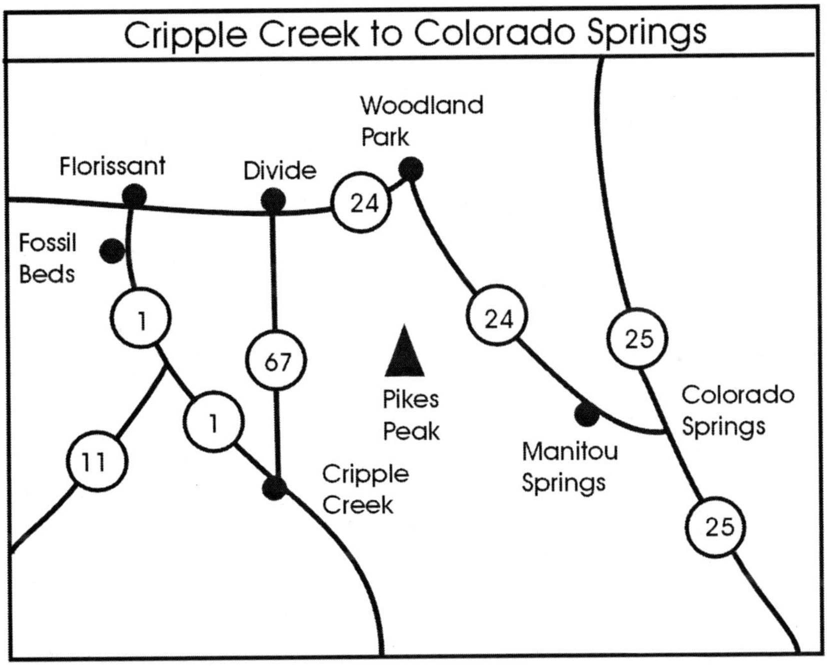

Florissant Fossil Beds

Are you ready for a change of pace? Trust us; this will be more enjoyable than it may sound at first. Between 80,000 and 100,000 people per year come here to view one of the world's most extensive and important fossil records as well as to enjoy a pleasant nature walk.

Colorado has some premier fossil sites. There are several others along our tour route: one north of Cañon City, one east of Cañon City and one near the Red Rocks Amphitheater outside Denver. We just couldn't go by another site without stopping. Especially this one.

The Florissant Fossil Beds National Monument is open year-round 9 am to 5 pm except Thanksgiving/end of November, Christmas and New

Years Days; 719-748-3253, *www.nps.gov/flfo*. Schedules of ranger programs and guided hikes are posted.

To get there, take Florissant Road/Teller County Road 1 at the western end of Bennett Avenue. (Turn right on B St. and left on Carr.) After 15 miles, you'll find the Florissant Fossil Beds National Monument on your left. If you've run out of time and need to bypass the fossil beds, head north from Cripple Creek 20 miles on Colorado 67 to Divide, then east 22 miles on US 24 to Manitou Springs or Colorado Springs, where we'll have dinner.

Here's a little background to whet your appetite: Fossils, as you know, are remnants or impressions of plants or animals that have been preserved in soft rock. Paleontologists study them in order to learn about past geological periods.

The fossils at Florissant Fossil Beds National Monument were laid down during the Eocene Epoch, from 55 to 34 million years ago. The area was once a near-tropical waterland teeming with fish, surrounded by more than 140 species of plants and buzzing with 1,400 species of insects. Volcanic eruptions over the centuries frequently sent tons of ash into the air. When it settled, the ash brought down and encapsulated insects, animals and plants. In addition, mudflows buried trees where they stood and their stumps were turned to stone as minerals gradually seeped into them.

Over time, the ash and mud became compressed into shale, was raised during the uplift of the Rockies and was eroded by rains, thereby uncovering the fossils that you'll see. The fossil beds were discovered in 1874 by a U.S. Geological Survey geologist and are the source of some 50,000 specimens that now reside in more than 20 museums and universities in the U.S. and the United Kingdom.

What is there to do here? Start in the visitor center where you'll see remarkably detailed specimens of familiar insects and plants that have been gathered from throughout the 6,000 acre site—beetles, bees, dragonflies, ants, spiders, butterflies; leaves from willow, maple, birch, beech and hickory trees; needles from fir and sequoia trees.

Then, ask for a copy of the hiking trails brochure and decide which of the 14 miles of trails you have the energy and time for. The 1.4 mile, self-guided Petrified Forest Loop (there is a separate pamphlet for this walk) features three petrified sequoia trunks that share a root system, and Big Stump, a petrified sequoia stump that measures 38 feet around. Big Stump is estimated to have been over 230 feet tall—that's about 23 stories high—making it a rival of the sequoias and redwoods in California.

The Woman Homesteader

Eight-tenths of a mile after you turn left out of the fossil beds parking lot, you'll come upon the Hornbek Homestead. On Fossil Beds Monument land, this property is a restoration by the National Park Service and well worth a brief visit. As was the case with us, you may experience another trip back in time—to the year 1878. (See the photograph at the beginning of this book.)

By 1878, 44-year-old Adeline Hornbek and her four children (Frank 18, Annie 17, George 14 and Elliott 7) had built a prosperous ranch with this main house as its focal point. (The other buildings were moved here from nearby historic ranches to represent the earlier bunkhouse, carriage shed and barn.)

The house was unusually large for its day. A typical pioneer home would fit inside Adeline's bedroom on the first floor of the house, and there are three bedrooms upstairs! The parlor was large enough that neighbors often came here for Saturday night dances. And Adeline must have enjoyed working in her very roomy kitchen. The well house was built onto the structure in 1909. All women should take heart from what you'll see and learn here.

Widow Adeline Hornbek took advantage of a provision in the Homestead Act of 1862 that allowed any head of family, man or woman, over 21 years of age to acquire 160 acres of free land if that person lived on and improved the land for a period of five years. Altogether, she lived here 27 years and is surely worthy of our admiration.

Born in Massachusetts, she came to Florissant via Oklahoma Territory and Denver. Red-haired and tall for the 1880's at 5'7", she must have had full measures of self-confidence and gumption to venture to the wilds with her children.

Adeline raised hay, as well as potatoes and garden vegetables that were stored in her hillside root cellar. She owned 21 horses, 4 milk cows, 100 beef cattle, 3 swine and 50 poultry.

The Hornbek Homestead's buildings are open daily between Memorial Day/late May and Labor Day/early September, but simply wandering the grounds is a good way to get a feel for life on a remote mountain homestead in the late 1800's.

Before we leave this lovely valley, were you wondering about the meaning of the word "florissant"? In French, it means "flowering." The valley was given that name by an early settler from Florissant, Missouri.

*****

Now, it's time to head toward the last major stop on our tour, Colorado Springs, which is just 36 miles away.

Two miles north of the Hornbek Homestead, you'll come to US 24, where you'll turn right and head east. Soon after you pass the town of Divide and Colorado 67, you'll enjoy a good view of Pikes Peak to your right. The 14,110-foot mountain will be in the background much of tomorrow as we enjoy our last day's activities.

Pikes Peak, you may already know, was named for Lieutenant Zebulon Pike who led a small expedition to within a short distance of the summit in 1806. You may also know that after seeing the "purple mountain majesties" from the top of Pikes Peak in 1893, Katherine Lee Bates wrote a poem which became the lyrics of "America the Beautiful," the song that many Americans think is, or should be, our national anthem.

Tomorrow, you may choose to enjoy that same view from the top after driving to the summit, or taking the Pikes Peak Cog Railway.

If it's the dinner hour as you approach Manitou Springs, consider stopping at one of our favorite restaurants in the area, the historic Stagecoach Inn at 702 Manitou Ave. Simply leave the highway at the first Manitou exit and you're practically there. After dinner, continue two streetlights farther on Manitou Ave., re-enter US 24 and drive to your overnight accommodations in Colorado Springs—unless they're in Manitou Springs, of course. See "It's Dinnertime!," below for other restaurant possibilities in Manitou Springs and Colorado Springs.

Speaking of eating, we strongly recommend, if you haven't done so already, that you make reservations by this evening for tomorrow's dinner at the Flying W Ranch (telephone 719-598-4000). They seat more than 1,000 people for their excellent chuck wagon supper and western show, but they fill up nearly every evening during the summer, and reservations are a must. Also, we recommend that you plan to be there no later than 5:15 pm; seats are assigned as you arrive and there is plenty to keep you occupied on the grounds until dinner is served at 7:15.

It's Dinnertime!

In Colorado Springs

- **Jake & Telly's**, Continental-Greek, casual fine dining, 2616 W. Colorado Ave., 719-633-0406, *www.greekdining.com*, $$.
- **Jose Muldoon's**, Mexican, casual, 222 N. Tejon St., 719-636-2311, no website, $$-$$.

- **La Petite Maison**, contemporary American, upscale casual, 1015 W. Colorado Ave., 719-632-4887, *www.restauranteur.com*/maison, $$-$$$.
- **MacKenzie's Chop House**, American, 1930's speakeasy, 128 S. Tejon St., 719-635-3536, *www.restauranteur.com/mackenzieschop housecom,* $$-$$$.
- **Phantom Canyon Brewing Co.**, American, pub atmosphere, 2 E. Pike's Peak, 719-635-2800, *www.phantomcanyon.com,* $.

In Manitou Springs

- **Adam's Mountain Cafe**, gourmet vegetarian, casual elegant, 110 Cañon Ave., 719-685-1430, *www.adamsmountain.com,* $$.
- **Briarhurst Manor**, wild game, fine dining, 404 Manitou Ave., 719-685-1864, *www.briarhurst.com*, $$$-$$$$.
- **Craftwood Inn**, wild game, English Tudor style, 404 El Paso Blvd., 719-685-9000, *www.craftwood.com*, $$$-$$$$.
- **Mona Lisa Fondue Restaurant**, fondue and four-course meals, cozy-intimate, 733 Manitou Ave., 719-685-0277, *www.monalisa fondue.com*, $$$$.
- **Stagecoach Inn**, diverse menu, casual, 702 Manitou Ave., 719-685-9400, *www.stagecoachinn.com*, $$-$$$.

Ginnodo-recommended B&Bs

- **Black Forest B&B Lodge and Cabins**, 11170 Black Forest Rd., Colorado Springs, CO 80908, 719-495-4208, 800-809-9901, fax 719-495-0688, *www.blackforestbb.com, blackforestbb@msn.com,* $$-$$$.
- **Cheyenne Cañon Inn**, 2030 W. Cheyenne Blvd., Colorado Springs 80906, 719-633-0625, 800-633-0625, fax 719-633-8826, *www. cheyennecanyoninn.com*, *info@cheyennecanoninn.com*, $$-$$$.
- **Holden House B&B Inn**, 1102 W. Pikes Peak Ave., Colorado Springs 80904, 719-471-3980, 888-565-3980, fax 719-471-4740, *www.holdenhouse.com*, *mail@holdenhouse.com*, $$.
- **The Inn at Cascade,** 4675 Hagerman Ave., Cascade 80809, 719-684-2194, 800-507-4030, *www.theinnatcascade.com, info@theinn atcascade.com,*
- **Old Town Guest House**, 115 S. 26th St., Colorado Springs 80904, 719-632-9194, 888-375-4210, fax 719-632-9026, *www.oldtown-guesthouse.com, luxury@oldtown-guesthouse.com,* $$-$$$.

- **Red Crags B&B Inn**, 302 El Paso Blvd., Manitou Springs 80829, 719-685-1920, 800-721-2248, fax 719-685-1073, *www.redcrags .com, info@redcrags.com,* $$-$$$.
- **Rocky Mountain Lodge and Cabins,** 4680 Hagerman Ave., Cascade 80809, 719-684-2521, 888-298-0348, *www.rocky mountainlodge.com, info@rockymountainlodge.com,* $$-$$$.
- **Room at the Inn**, 618 N. Nevada Ave., Colorado Springs 80903, 719-442-1896, 888-442-1896, fax 719-442-6802, *www.roomatthe inn.com, rooms@roomattheinn.com,* $$.
- **Victoria's Keep**, 202 Ruxton Ave., Manitou Springs 80829, 719-685-5354, 800-905-5337, fax 719-685-5913, *www.victoriaskeep .com, info@victoriaskeep.com,* $-$$$.
- **More B&Bs at** *www.pikespeakareabnbs.com*, *www.innsofcolo rado.org*, and *www.colorado-bnb.com.*

AAA- or Mobil-recommended Motels/Hotels

- **Antlers Hilton Colorado Springs**, 4 S. Cascade Ave., Colorado Springs 80903, 719-955-5600, fax 719-389-0259, *www.antlers.com,* $$$.
- **The Broadmoor**, 1 Lake Ave., Colorado Springs 80906, 719-634-7711, 866-837-9520, fax 719-577-5738, *www.broadmoor.com*, $$$-$$$$.
- **Garden of the Gods Motel**, 2922 W. Colorado Ave., Colorado Springs 80904, 719-636-5271, 800-637-0703 fax 719-477-1422, *http://gardenofthegodsmotel.pikes-peak.com*, $.
- **Holiday Inn Express-Air Force Academy,** 7110 Commerce Center Dr., Colorado springs 80919, 719-592-9800, 800-HOLIDAY, fax 719-593-9644, *www.ichotelsgroup.com*, $$.
- **LaQuinta Inn Garden of the Gods**, 4385 Sinton Rd., Colorado Springs 80907, 719-528-5060, 800-531-5900, fax 719-598-0360, *www.lq.com*, $-$$.
- **Rodeway Inn & Suites Garden of the Gods**, 555 W. Garden of the Gods Rd., Colorado Springs 80907, 719-593-9119, fax 719-260-0381, *www.choicehotels.com*, $$.

Woodall's-recommended RV Parks & Campgrounds

- **Fountain Creek RV Park:** Colorado Springs; from jct I-25 (exit 141) & US 24W, go 3 mi W on US 24, then 1 block N on 31st St., then 1/2 block E on Colorado Ave; 719-633-2192, *www.fountain creekrvpark.com.*

- **Garden of the Gods Campground:** Colorado Springs; from jct I-25 & US 24 (exit 141), go 2-1/2 mi W on US 24, then 1 block N on 31st St., then 6 blocks W on Colorado Ave to Columbia; 800-248-9451, *www.coloradocampground.com, camp@coloradocampground.com.*
- **Golden Eagle Ranch Campground & RV Park:** Colorado Springs; from I-25, take exit 135 W (toward the mountains) to Hwy 115 S, then go 5 mi S on Hwy 115 (Nevada Ave) to big campground sign, then 1 mi W; 800-666-3841.
- **Goldfield RV Park:** Colorado Springs; from jct I-25 (exit 141) & US 24, go 2 mi W on US 24, then 50 feet S on 26th St; 888-471-0495, *www.goldfieldrvcampground.com.*
- **KOA-Colorado Springs South:** Fountain; from jct I-25 & Hwy 16 (exit 132), go 100 feet E on Hwy 16, then 1 mi S on frontage road; 719-382-7575.
- **Lone Duck Campground:** Cascade; from jct I-25 & US 24, go 12 mi W on US 24; 800-776-5925.
- **Mountaindale Campground & Cabins:** Colorado Springs; from jct I-25 & US 24, go 5 mi S on I-25 to Academy (exit 135), then 15 mi S on SR115, then 2 mi W on Barrett; 719-576-0619, *www.mountaindalecampground.com, mountaindalecamp@msn.com.*
- **Pikes Peak RV Park Campground:** Manitou Springs; from jct US 24 & Business-24 (Manitou Ave), go ¼ mi W on Manitou Ave; 800-685-9409.
- **Rocky Top Motel & RV Park:** Green Mountain Falls; from jct I-25 & US 24, go 16 mi N on US 24; 719-684-9044.
- **Wrangler RV Ranch & Motel:** Colorado Springs; from jct I-25 & US 24, go 4 mi E on US 24 to Powers (US 24E), then 2 mi N on Powers to Platte Ave; 719-591-1402.

Day Seven: The Springs

This chapter's title is a bit of a misnomer, because there are no springs in Colorado Springs. But there are 26 mineral springs in nearby Manitou Springs, and they provided the inspiration for the naming of Colorado's second largest city.

As with greater Denver, the Colorado Springs area has many activities to happily occupy the traveler for days. And, as with the Denver area, we've selected the ones that we believe you'll most enjoy today. They include visits to: beautiful and interesting Seven Falls; your choice of a Native American museum or a museum focused on the American cowboy; the Air Force Academy with its stunning Cadet Chapel; the Garden of the Gods, in mid- to late-afternoon when the sun is shining on the western side of the red rocks; and dinner at the Flying W Ranch, which is as much a vacation destination as it is a place to eat and be entertained.

(Be forewarned that you may not have enough time to return to your accommodations between the Garden of the Gods and the Flying W Ranch, which are geographically close to one another.)

If one or more of those doesn't appeal to you, we've provided information on other popular activities at the end of this chapter. They include Cave of the Winds, Cheyenne Mountain Zoo, Colorado Springs Fine Arts Center, Glen Eyrie Castle, Pikes Peak Cog Railway, Pioneers Museum, Van Briggle Art Pottery Studio, U.S. Olympic Training Center, and the Western Museum of Mining and Industry.

Town Father and Railroad Tycoon

Before we begin our day, let's have a brief encounter with the man who dominated Colorado Springs' early history, General William Jackson Palmer. We've already introduced you to another former resident, Winfield Scott Stratton, discoverer of the Independence Mine in Cripple Creek. Other residents you may have heard of include: Spencer Penrose, who was also prominent in mining and was the builder of Colorado Springs' Broadmoor Hotel; Helen Hunt Jackson, a writer (*Ramona*), poet and champion of Indian rights; and Chief Ouray who apparently spent winters here with his Ute Indian tribesmen.

After serving as one of the youngest Union generals in the Civil War, William Jackson Palmer worked on the Kansas Pacific Railroad survey and fell in love with this land at the foot of Pikes Peak. A man of vision and energy, he built the Denver and Rio Grande Railroad, which

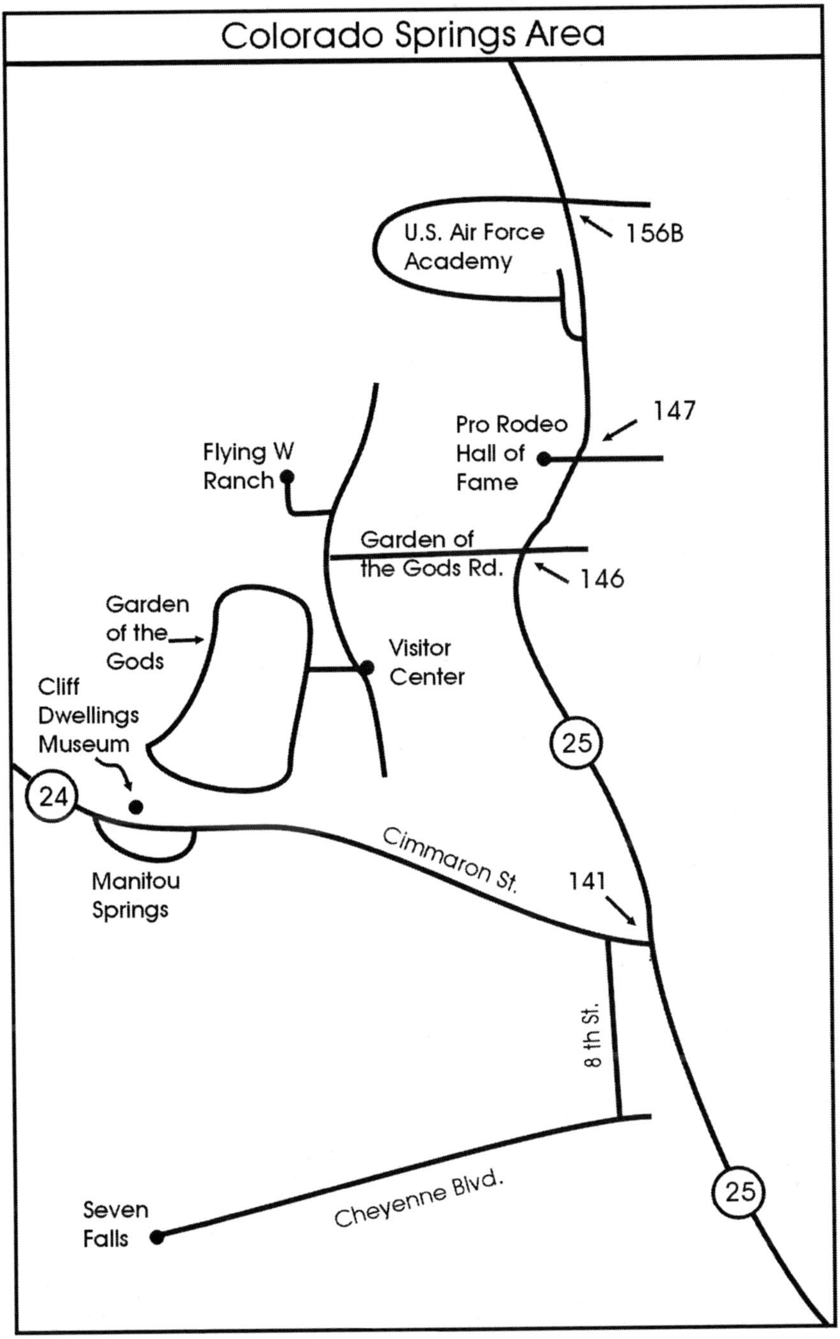
Colorado Springs Area
U.S. Air Force Academy
156B
147
Pro Rodeo Hall of Fame
Flying W Ranch
Garden of the Gods Rd.
146
Garden of the Gods
Visitor Center
Cliff Dwellings Museum
25
24
Cimmaron St.
141
Manitou Springs
8 th St.
Cheyenne Blvd.
Seven Falls
25

was a moving force (pun intended) in Colorado mining and transportation history. And in 1871, he purchased more than 9,000 acres of land, had the streets of downtown Colorado Springs laid out, and sold house, business and farm lots to the first residents of the area.

It was Palmer's Denver and Rio Grande Railroad that laid the tracks through the Royal Gorge and carried ore, supplies and people to and from Leadville and many other mining communities.

A practical and hard-nosed businessman, Palmer could also be caring and generous. During the Civil War, he befriended a runaway slave boy, making him an orderly. He gave jobs to unfortunates who needed them. Upon his retirement from the railroad, he traveled to each of his stations, handing out a total of $1 million in cash as thank-you gifts to his workers. And following a horseback riding accident which paralyzed him and made him unable to travel back East for a reunion of his old army unit, he brought the entire regiment to Colorado Springs by train and feted them here, all expenses paid.

Seven Falls

There's more to this attraction than the name implies. Yes, there are seven falls to see, but we believe you'll be absorbed in wildlife during most of your time here, as we were. And, if you want some exercise, there's a nice walking trail at the top of the falls.

To get there, drive south on Interstate 25 to Exit 141, go west on US 24/Cimmaron St. to the first stop light where you'll turn left on 8th St., drive two miles to Cheyenne Blvd., then turn right and drive two miles to Seven Falls. This attraction is open from 8:30 am to 9:30 pm from mid-May through the beginning of September, from 9 am to 5:15 pm during spring and fall, and 9 am to 4:15 during winter, except Thursdays during January and February when the attraction is closed; 719-632-0765, *www.sevenfalls.com.*

Seven Falls is situated in a box canyon; Native Americans used to trap animals by stampeding them into its dead-end. The beauty of the falls, which cascade 300 feet down the granite cliff, is undeniable. You can enjoy them from the bottom, from the top by climbing the 265 stairs, and from the Eagles Nest by taking the elevator to the observation platform.

We spent a lot of our time here feeding the chipmunks (with peanuts from the dispensers on the side of the snack bar), watching the trout, and reading the three wonderfully descriptive displays featuring the animals, birds and trees of the area. Native American dances are performed here during the summer. This is a fun and relaxing way to start the day.

Indians or Cowboys?

We found it hard to choose between the two museums that we're now going to describe, so we leave the choice to you.

The **Manitou Cliff Dwellings Museum** is the re-creation of an Anasazi cliff dwelling that was relocated from Southwestern Colorado in 1904 by archeologists to preserve the evidence of a prehistoric culture. The Anasazi were prominent in the Four Corners area (where Colorado, New Mexico, Arizona and Utah meet) until about the year 1300 when they mysteriously disappeared as a tribal entity. Whether because of drought, the pressure of enemy tribes, or some other reason, they were apparently absorbed by the Hopi and Zuni tribes in Arizona and New Mexico.

These dwellings are an example of what you would see on a larger scale if you traveled to Mesa Verde National Park near Durango, Colorado, or to other Anasazi ruins farther south and west. So, unless you plan a trip to the Four Corners area, this may be your one shot at examining an extinct Native American culture.

What you'll see here, under a sandstone overhang in Phantom Cliff Canyon, are 40 representative Anasazi rooms, including sleeping quarters, a lookout tower and a ceremonial structure called a kiva. The museum also contains a "pueblo," a three-story building similar to ones occupied by today's Native Americans in Taos, New Mexico. In one room of the pueblo, you'll find dioramas depicting Anasazi life and a display of cliff-dweller artifacts that were gathered from throughout the Southwest, including pottery, tools, weapons, burial urns and jewelry. Native American folk dancers perform outside during the summer months.

The Manitou Cliff Dwellings Museum is open seven days a week, year-round: May through September from 9 am to 6 pm; December through February from 10 am to 4 pm; March, April, October and November from 9 am to 5 pm; 719-685-5242, 800-354-9971, *www.cliffdwellingsmuseum.com*. To get there, drive west on US 24 to Manitou Springs, and take the Cliff Dwellings Road exit.

For lunch, try **Breadheads** at 729 Manitou Ave. (719-685-2400) or **Adams Mountain Cafe** at 111 Cañon Ave. (719-685-1430)—both in Manitou Springs, a block apart.

On the cowboy side, we suggest the **ProRodeo Hall of Fame and Museum of the American Cowboy**. To get there, drive north on Interstate 25 to exit 147, turn left at the stoplight onto Rockrimmon Blvd., and left again onto ProRodeo Drive. This attraction is open daily from 9 am to 5 pm April through August, and Thursday through Sunday

9 am to 5 pm September through March. 101 ProRodeo Dr., Colorado Springs 80919; 719-528-4764, *http://prorodeo.org/hof.*

This is a classy operation. If you have even a little interest in, or curiosity about, cowboy life and rodeo, you will enjoy the comprehensive and elegant way in which they are presented here.

Start by viewing the multi-media presentation that depicts the history of cowboys and rodeos in the West. Following that, you'll be guided to Heritage Hall, which has displays of historic and modern cowboy, and rodeo gear, including saddles, ropes, chaps, clothing, boots and hats. After that, there is a movie in a second theater showing live rodeo action, including a ride on a Brahma bull...from the top of the bull.

Then, tour the Hall of Champions where—as with other sports halls of fame—you'll see photographs, equipment, trophies, personal memorabilia and records of these unique American athletes. Professional rodeo is the only major spectator sport to have evolved from a working lifestyle. There are also lots of great photographs, as well as western sculptures and paintings, to be enjoyed. The tooled western saddles are themselves works of art.

There are two other things worth seeing here. Don't miss the panoramic rodeo arena in the far left corner of the Hall of Champions, where you can walk into the center of the ring and experience the sights and sounds of the rodeo. And outside, just off the patio, you'll find a replica rodeo arena, and live rodeo animals during the summer.

What to do about lunch? We suggest that you drive one exit south on I-25 to Garden of the Gods Road and eat at **Black Eyed Pea**, which you'll see on your left as you come off the exit. You'll find other restaurants to choose from in the same area.

Air Force Academy

The Cadet Chapel at the U.S. Air Force Academy is the most-visited man-made structure in Colorado, for good reason, as you'll see. And the Visitor Center does an excellent job of enlightening the public about cadet and college life on this campus that opened in 1958.

To get to the Air Force Academy's North Entrance, drive north on Interstate 25 to exit 156B and then west toward the Rampart Range. Follow the signs to the Visitor Center, passing the B52 display and the Field House on your left.

After parking, we suggest that you first walk about five minutes to the Cadet Chapel via the trail at the right of the Visitor Center. As you approach the Chapel, take note of the cluster of buildings that nearly encircle it. They comprise the heart of the campus: the classrooms, dormitories, dining hall, library, social center, planetarium, headquarters and parade grounds.

Following are the highlights of the Cadet Chapel, as taken mostly from the brochure that can be found at the entrance to the Protestant Chapel. This building is, of course, a place of worship, but what draws visitors here is that it is also a stunning architectural accomplishment (see the photograph at the beginning of this book) and a repository of beautiful religious art.

Walter A. Netsch, Jr. of the Skidmore, Owings and Merrill architectural firm, Chicago, designed the building. It took five years of planning and four years of construction and was completed in the summer of 1963. The design is unique not only because of its 17 striking 150-foot silvery spires and its elegant interior furnishings, but also because it contains three chapels under one roof, each with its own entrance. (They are all uniquely beautiful; we suggest that you visit all three, in the order that follows.)

Entered from the terrace level on the east and west sides, the Jewish Chapel seats 100 in comfortable walnut armchairs. From left to right, behind the pulpit, you will see: the Menorah, or traditional seven-branched candelabra; the Holy Ark, which shelters the Torah; the Eternal Light, suspended from the ceiling; the Kiddish Cup and two candlesticks; and the Holocaust Torah Scroll, which was hidden from the Nazi's during WWII. The paintings on the southern and northern walls, completed in 1985 and 1986 by Israeli painter, Shlomo Katz, depict brotherhood and justice; and those on the western wall were painted by Katz in honor of the Air Force.

The Catholic Chapel, seating 500 worshipers, is also entered from the terrace level, but from the south. The two marble sculptures on the front wall—Our Lady of the Skies and the Guardian Angel—help direct the eye to the spread-winged dove, symbolic of the Holy Spirit, and the six-foot sculptured nickel silver Crucifix by Lumen Martin Winter. The background is made of Venetian glass tessera and is an abstract portrayal of the firmament. The 14 Stations of the Cross located on the east and west walls were also sculpted by Mr. Winter; their marble comes from the same quarries that Michelangelo used in his work, and the small olivewood cross in each work comes from the Mount Of Olives in Jerusalem. The needlepoint kneelers along the Communion Rail were made by individual members of the Air Force Officers' Wives Clubs.

Also located on this lower level is the All Faiths Room, just north of the Jewish Chapel. It is the worship area for smaller religious meetings and is purposely devoid of religious symbolism.

The 1,200-seat Protestant Chapel is entered from the south. The first glimpse of the vaulted interior, suffused with multi-colored shafts of light, is breathtaking. The side and upper walls are the soaring spires that you saw outside. There are 24 shades of stained glass (24,000 pieces) between the spires, with darker colors in the back of the chapel and lighter colors in the front—suggesting that worshipers are coming into God's light.

The beautifully-crafted marble altar and pulpit are positioned in front of a crescent-shaped mosaic wall, above which hangs a 46-foot aluminum cross which appears to float and to appear and disappear depending on the viewer's angle. The kneelers along the Communion Rail were made by individual members of the Air Force Officer's Wives Clubs. In the rear of the chapel, seemingly suspended above the choir loft, is the 4,334-pipe Protestant Chapel Organ, one of the most magnificent displays of pipe work in our country.

The Cadet Chapel is open Monday through Saturday from 9 am to 5 pm. and Sunday from 1 pm to 5 pm, but is occasionally closed for special services. The Visitor Center is open seven days a week from 9 am to 5 pm, except major holidays; 719-333-2025, *www.usafa.af.mil.*

As you enter the Visitor Center, we would encourage you to consider how much time you have available to take in its details. If you want to fully enjoy Colorado Springs' number one attraction, the Garden of the Gods, and be in position at 5:30 pm for good seating at the Flying W Ranch, you should leave here about 2:30 pm.

A worthwhile 12-minute movie, "The Academy Challenge," shows every half hour. The Visitors Center also contains informative exhibits on cadet life and about the Academy, both past and present. If you want to take home Air Force accessory items to children or friends, you'll find plenty in the gift shop.

When you're ready to head off to the Garden of the Gods, turn left out of the Visitors Center parking lot, follow Academy Drive to Stadium Blvd. where you'll turn right. Then turn left onto Southgate Blvd. and exit the Academy onto Interstate 25 toward Colorado Springs. As you drive along Southgate Blvd., you'll see the Thunderbird Airmanship Overlook where you may observe parachuting, soaring and powered flight.

Garden of the Gods

Turn off Interstate 25 at Exit 146 and drive west for two miles on Garden of the Gods Road to 30th Street, where you'll turn left. (Before this junction, take note of the sign that tells you to turn the opposite direction on 30th Street to get to the Flying W Ranch.) Just 1.4 miles from that intersection, you'll come upon the entrance to Garden of the Gods Park on your right. (See the photograph on the back cover of this book.) The park is open from 5 am to 11 pm from May through October and 5 am to 9 pm the rest of the year.

But before you enter the park, we suggest that you turn left into the Visitor and Nature Center and spend a half hour there. Be sure to see the excellent 12-minute multi-media show titled, "How Did Those Red Rocks Get There?" Also look for (and manipulate) the Rocks of the Garden display, as well as see the adjoining description of how the continents moved about 200 million years ago. Open daily year-round, from 9 am to 5 pm, except closed Tuesdays in January and February. 1805 N. 30th St., Colorado Springs 80904; 719-634-6666, *www.gardenofgods.com.*

Are you ready for another visual feast? (See the photograph at the beginning of this book.) If the sun is shining—and it does so about 300 days a year in Colorado Springs—you'll want to take out that camera and turn on your memory machine. Early morning sun on the eastern side of the red rocks is beautiful, but we think the afternoon sun on the western side is spectacular.

From the main entrance to this free 1,360-acre city park, follow the road to the right 0.7 mile to the Main North Parking Lot (on the left) where you'll leave your car and take the path down past Kissing Camels Rock on your right and White Rock on your left. After passing between Sentinel Rock and North and South Gateway Rocks, turn right and follow the easy, 3/4-mile loop trail that takes you past the foot of the park's tallest rock formations—those already mentioned, plus, in the order you'll see them, Tower of Babel, Pulpit Rock, Three Graces and Cathedral Spires.

The trail also provides excellent rock viewing from a distance as well. Along the way, see if you can identify the abundant Gambel oak tree, also known as scrub oak, which has a small, typical oak-shaped leaf and is usually less than 15 feet tall.

Every time we've been here, we've enjoyed watching technical climbers using ropes to work their way up and down the rocks. They must obtain special permits from the Visitors Center in order to climb.

How did these stunning red sandstone formations come to be? If you guessed that they popped up out of the ground, you're basically correct. Geologists believe that about 300 million years ago, they were deposited as sediment in rivers and as sand in seawater and that they became compressed over time into sandstone. Then, when the Rocky Mountains uplifted about 65 million years ago, they were broken and thrust upward from a horizontal to a vertical position. Some have also been moved sideways from their original positions as a result of faulting in the earth. Since then, they have been eroded by rain, wind, freezing and thawing to their current shapes...and the erosion and faulting continues.

Are you also wondering why most of the rocks are red and why White Rock is white? The difference is in the amount of iron minerals present in the rock. White Rock has almost no iron and has not "rusted" like the red rocks. Geologists theorize that before the rocks were solidified and tilted up, water flowing through the White Rock deposit leached away the iron minerals.

Next, we'd like to show you a very different rock formation. But don't miss the great photo opportunity that's just around the corner! About 1/4 mile after you leave the parking lot, pull into the five-space pullout on your left and get that award-winning picture that you've always thought you could take. Then, keeping to the right, continue on Ridge Road/Garden Drive for 1.5 miles until you come to Balanced Rock.

This time, if you guessed that Balanced Rock fell from the sky or somehow rolled here to its resting position, you'd be wrong. The explanation is that the rock beneath it is softer and has eroded; leaving Balanced Rock in a somewhat suspended state.

Now, with the time remaining here, we're going to present you with another difficult choice. Actually, three choices. The first is to explore the park some more and find a spot that particularly appeals to you; then hike or simply soak up the beauty. The second is to shop at the Trading Post. And the third is to visit Rockledge Ranch. If you're enjoying yourself and don't much care about getting to the Flying W Ranch by 5:30 for good seating, by all means spend more time on one of these activities.

The **Trading Post** is back along the road you came and just around the corner to the right. It bills itself as "traditionally the oldest, certainly the largest and clearly the best, gift shop and art gallery in the Pikes Peak region." We would agree that this is THE place in the area to see and purchase authentic Native American arts, crafts and jewelry, and to find quality souvenirs and gifts to take home. Open all year: summer from 8 am to 8 pm; winter from 9 am to 5:30 pm; 800-874-4515; *www.co-trading-post.com.*

Rock Ledge Ranch Historic Site, just inside the main entrance to the Garden of the Gods, gives you the opportunity to examine farm life in three different pioneer eras—the Homestead Period (1872), the Ranch Era (1895) and the Estate Period (1907). Actors in period costumes will show you how Coloradans worked and lived back then, including demonstrations of blacksmithing and agricultural techniques. Open Wednesday through Sunday, 10 am to 5 pm from June through Labor Day. 1401 Recreation Way, Colorado Springs 80905; 719-578-6777, *www.rockledgeranch.com, rlr@rockledgeranch .com.*

Are you ready to eat, tap your feet and have an all-around good time? Then let's head off to the Flying W Ranch by retracing our route on 30th Street and driving past Garden of the Gods Road to the first left, which is Flying W Ranch Road. If you wish to opt out of the meal and entertainment at the Flying W Ranch, consult the restaurant listing at the end of Day Six.

The Flying W Ranch – A Food and Fun Destination

We don't know about you, but we've been looking forward to this all day. We've enjoyed the food, the show, the old western town, the shops and the ambiance immensely every time we've come here. You may be browsing, chowing and spectating with more than 1,000 other people, but the pace is easy and the mood is light.

During summer, the gates open at 4:30 pm. Arrival by 5:30 is recommended for first come-first served seating, dinner is served at 7:15, and the show starts about 8:30. During the month of September, the gates open at 5 pm, dinner is served at 6:45, and the show starts at 8. Payment is by cash, traveler's checks, MasterCard or Visa. Advance reservations, preferably several days ahead, are a must for most evenings during the summer; they'll be held until 7 pm. 3330 Chuckwagon Road, Colorado Springs 809191; 800-232-FLYW, 719-598-4000, *www.flyingw.com.*

(The Flying W Steakhouse is open on Friday and Saturday evenings, October through December and March through mid-May. The Steakhouse menu is more extensive, and, as you might guess, the Flying W Wranglers put on a show after dinner.)

You'll want to wander the grounds while waiting for dinner to be served, and will notice, of course, that the backdrop of the ranch is an extension of the rock formations that you saw in the Garden of the Gods. You'll also notice that, as an historical presentation, the western town, with its 14 restored buildings and antique contents, doesn't quite measure up to South Park City in Fairplay. But the buildings and shops are interesting and fun, and the items for sale are of good quality.

Be sure to visit the pueblo building to observe Indian blanket weaving, and the blacksmith shop to see a horseshoeing demonstration between 6 and 7 pm. We also particularly enjoyed the Church, the Old Jail, and Irene's Homestead.

You'll be pleasantly surprised at the efficient way that the Flying W manages to feed more than 1,000 people and get things cleaned up in less than an hour. Having done this since 1953, they've gotten the details down pretty well. Going through the serving line and having your chuck wagon supper plopped onto your tin plate is part of the fun. It consists of sliced beef or barbecued chicken, baked potato, Flying W beans, the best chunky applesauce and biscuits you'll ever eat, spice cake and a choice of coffee, lemonade or iced tea. This is a very tasty and filling meal!

Then settle back for a very enjoyable hour of music and laughter. (See the photograph at the beginning of this book.) You'll hear some familiar western songs and some that are new to you. And you'll find the humor to be both laid-back and tasteful. The Flying W Wranglers are true professionals with more than 30 albums to their credit. The Flying W website claims, "No brag, just fact, this is the very best western stage show in the world." And we believe it! This show will surely be a highlight of your trip.

Wasn't that a great way to finish off our seven perfect days in Colorado?

Accommodations

See the lists of recommended B&Bs, motels, hotels and campgrounds at the end of Day Six.

Tomorrow

After overnighting in Colorado Springs, all you need to do is drive north 1-1/2 hours to Denver on Interstate 25, turn off either at Exit 194 (toll road E470) or at Exit 200 (Interstate 225 to Interstate 70) and follow the signs to the airport. The map on page 5 may be helpful as you enter the Denver area.

*****

ALTERNATIVE ACTIVITIES

During our tour, we've had the experience of being above treeline in Rocky Mountain National Park and of enjoying a spectacular view from the "Roof of the Rockies." That's why traveling to the top of Pikes Peak isn't on the seven-day tour. However, if we had time for only the four-day southern portion of the tour, we would spend the morning in Colorado Springs taking the Pikes Peak Cog Railway, or the toll road, to the top of the most famous mountain in the Rockies. (We would not do so if we had heart or respiratory problems, or do it on the prior afternoon, because it's wise to let your body begin to acclimate to the altitude before making such an ascent. We'd use the prior afternoon to visit Seven Falls and either the Cliff Dwellings or the ProRodeo Hall of Fame.)

Since preferences in vacation activities do differ significantly between people, we're listing here some that you may wish to pursue instead of the ones we've chosen. Some of the descriptions are excerpted from the city's Official Visitor Guide which can be obtained from the Colorado Springs Convention and Visitors Bureau, 104 S. Cascade, Suite 104, 80903; 719-635-7506 (out of state tel: 800-DO-VISIT), *www.experiencecoloradosprings.com.*

Cave of the Winds

You'll walk through a spectacular network of rooms and passageways encrusted with beautiful stalactites, stalagmites and flowstone curtains. Guided tours are available every day from 9 am to 9 pm during the summer and from 10 am to 5 pm during the winter. Drive six miles west of Colorado Springs on US 24 to Cave of the Winds Road; 719-685-5444, *www.caveofthewinds.com.*

Cheyenne Mountain Zoo

You will see over 500 diverse and exotic creatures. Highlights include Primate World, a habitat for great apes and monkeys, Wolf Woods, a mountainside habitat for Mexican wolves, and a monument to one of America's greatest humorists, Will Rogers. Open from 9 am to 6 pm Memorial Day/late May through Labor Day/early September, and 9 am to 5 pm the rest of the year. Exit 138 off I-25, drive west toward the mountains and follow the signs; 719-633-9925, *www.cmzoo.org, info@cmzoo.org.*

Colorado Springs Fine Arts Center

Enjoy paintings and sculptures by John James Audubon, Albert Bierstadt, Georgia O'Keefe, Charles Russell, John Singer Sargent and others, as well as an excellent collection of Native American and Hispanic art. There is also a sculpture garden and a tactile gallery where you're encouraged to touch the art. Open 9 am to 5 pm Monday through Saturday, 10 am to 5 pm Sunday. 30 W. Dale St. 80903; 719-634-5581, *www.csfineartscenter.org, info@csfineartscenter.org.*

Colorado Springs Pioneers Museum

Learn about Colorado Springs' beginnings and about the railroad and mining era; see the reconstructed home and possessions of writer/Indian activist Helen Hunt Jackson; enjoy exhibits of quilts, antique Van Briggle pottery, firearms, Native American artifacts, turn-of-the-century toys, and clothing; ride the 90-year-old bird-cage elevator to the restored courtroom where several Perry Mason programs were filmed; learn about explorer Zebulon Pike. Located in the historic El Paso County Courthouse. Open Tuesday through Saturday 10 am to 5 pm year-round, Sunday 1 pm to 5 pm June through August. Free admission. 215 S. Tejon St.; 719-385-5990, *www.cspm.org. cosmuseum @springsgov.com.*

Glen Eyrie Castle

This was the estate of General William Jackson Palmer, founder of Colorado Springs and the Denver and Rio Grande Railroad. Tours of Glen Eyrie are provided by the Navigators, a Christian missionary organization, which owns the property and uses it as a headquarters and conference center. Guided tours of the circa-1906 castle are conducted daily at 1 pm, May-September; reservations are required. Access to the grounds is permitted from 9 am to 4 pm, Monday through Thursday. PO Box 6819, Colorado Springs 80934, 3820 N. 30th St., Colorado Springs 80904; 719-634-0808 or 800-944-4536, *www.gleneyrie.org.*

Manitou & Pike's Peak Cog Railway (and Highway)

The Swiss-made trains climb nine miles from a starting elevation of 6,571 ft. to 14,110 ft. at the summit. You'll see Denver 75 miles to the north, the Sangre de Cristo Mountains and New Mexico to the south, mile upon mile of snow-capped peaks to the west, and Colorado Springs and the vast expanse of plains stretching to Kansas in the east. The round trip takes three hours and ten minutes, including 30 to 40 minutes on the summit, Reservations in advance are strongly suggested at all times, and you must arrive ½ hour before your reserved departure time to purchase tickets. Be sure to have a jacket or sweater, even in summer! The railway operates year-round, but on a very limited schedule off peak. During summer, trains depart (if scheduled; be sure to check) at 8, 9:20, 10:40 am, 12 noon, and 1:20, 2:40, 4 and 5:20 pm. Travel west on US 24, take the Manitou Springs exit, drive west on Manitou Avenue for 1-1/2 miles and turn left onto Ruxton. There are also a hiking trail and a toll road (19 miles) to the top of Pikes Peak. The toll road starts in Cascade, 15 miles west of Colorado Springs on US 24. PO Box 351, 515 Ruxton Ave., Manitou Springs 80829; 719-685-5401, *www.cograilway.com, info@cograilway.com.*

U.S. Olympic Training Center

Tour the facilities where thousands of Olympic hopefuls train for more than 20 sports such as swimming, men's gymnastics, triathlon, volleyball, badminton, figure skating, speed skating, cycling, wrestling, weight lifting, shooting, and tae kwan do. Open year-around, 9 am to 5 pm, Monday through Saturday, and 11 am to 6 pm Sunday. Tours are conducted Monday through Saturday, each hour beginning at 9 am (last tour 4 pm; none on Sunday), and include a film about Olympic competition. Free admission and tours, except for some demonstrations and competitions. 1750 E. Boulder St., Colorado Springs, 719-578-4618 for visitor center, 719-866-4656 for reservations, *www.usoc.org/12181_19092.htm.*

Van Briggle Pottery

Enjoy a free tour, during which you'll see potters producing original pieces, as well as etching and glazing artists finishing and refining each piece by hand in the traditional manner begun here more than 100 years ago. You'll also see designs from Art Nouveau to current Southwestern styles, and figurines, Native American busts, bowls, vases, lamps and distinctive lampshades. You will, of course, be encouraged to purchase. Open 8:30 am to 5 pm, Monday through Saturday, and 12 noon to 5 pm on Sunday. Tours throughout the day, except Sunday. Located just five minutes west of downtown Colorado Springs at 21st Street and US 24. PO Box 96, Colorado Springs 80901; 719-633-7729, 1-800-847-6341, *www.vanbriggle.com, info@vanbriggle.com.*

Western Museum of Mining and Industry

Via indoor and outdoor displays, you'll see the actual operation of multi-ton steam engines, drills, hoists, locomotives and other carefully restored mining machines. You'll also learn to pan for gold and see how turn-of-the-century miners timbered, drilled, blasted, mucked and moved ore from the mine to the stamp mill, where ore was crushed and processed. Open from 9 am to 4 pm Monday through Saturday year-round (9am to 5 pm June-August). Daily guided tours at 10 am and 1 pm. Across from the Air Force Academy at exit 156A of Interstate 25. 225 North Gate Blvd., Colorado Springs 80921; 719-488-0880, 800-752-6558, *www.wmmi.org, info@wmmi.org.*

What to Wear, What to Bring

We have four words of advice about packing. First, be prepared for the season and be ready to put on or take off layers of clothing as necessary. Second, pack as little as possible; most people take more clothing than they need and end up hauling too many heavy suitcases. Third, consider using smaller suitcases with wheels and pull-handles. And, fourth, a list of things we believe are particularly important or that you might not think to bring along:

- A warm jacket, heavy sweater or sweatshirt, and long pants for the higher elevations and cool nights
- Rain gear
- Comfortable walking or hiking shoes that have been well broken-in
- A wide-brim hat and sunglasses with ultra-violet protection, because the sun is more intense at higher elevations
- A camera, to capture those special scenes, animals or moments
- Binoculars, especially to see wildlife up close
- A small first aid kit, to take care of potential blisters, cuts, headaches, colds and heartburn, plus a thermometer and tweezers
- Prescription medications, plus physician names and telephone numbers
- Telephone numbers of other emergency contacts (family and friends; also, leave your itinerary/phone numbers with them)
- A needle and thread, for emergency clothing repairs
- A pocket or Swiss Army knife with a can opener, also for emergencies
- A flashlight with fresh batteries, to help you get around at night in unfamiliar surroundings
- A compass, insect repellent, sun screen, lip salve, matches, toilet paper, fanny pack, and canteen or strap-on water bottle, if you plan to hike
- Dress-up clothes, if you intend to dine in upscale restaurants; otherwise, you can forget them

For Your Health and Safety

With a little knowledge and common sense you can prevent the health and safety problems that could spoil a great vacation. Only a small percentage of travelers experience these problems; we don't want you among them. As our mothers always said, "Forewarned is forearmed!" We are not doctors, but this accumulated wisdom that we've compiled from various sources and our own experience may be helpful.

Altitude sickness, also known as acute mountain sickness, is caused by decreasing atmospheric pressure. That is, the higher you go in the mountains, the harder your heart, lungs, and body tissues must work to draw in oxygen. Symptoms include: a hammering headache, nausea, dizziness, fatigue, rapid heartbeat, shortness of breath, sleeplessness and loss of appetite. *Prevention*: fast-walk, every day for 30 minutes, two to three weeks before you leave home; spend 24 hours or more in Denver or Colorado Springs (5,000-6,000 feet) at the beginning of your trip tok help your body acclimate to the altitude; avoid over-exertion during the entire trip.

But it's possible that you may experience one or more of the symptoms when you travel at elevations above 7,000 feet. If you do feel ill, especially if you have heart or nervous system problems, stop immediately and descend more than 1,000 feet to a lower altitude. If your symptoms are mild, drink lots of water, rest awhile to give your body a chance to adapt, take the headache medicine that's in your first aid kit, avoid alcohol and cigarettes, and eat lightly and frequently.

Cardiac patients should consult with their doctors prior to the trip, and proceed with special caution in the mountains.

Dehydration, as you know, is excessive loss of water from the body tissues, which can cause fever, diarrhea, vomiting and acidosis. It can sneak up on you in Colorado because the dry climate is so comfortable, and because water evaporates from the body more quickly. *Prevention*: increase your fluid intake (not alcohol), even when you don't feel thirsty.

Giardia, unlike dehydration, is something you may not have heard about. It's a microscopic organism found in lakes and streams, which can cause diarrhea, cramps, bloating and weight loss. *Prevention*: don't drink the water in those crystal-clear streams and lakes—unless it's been boiled for at least five minutes or you use a water filter system that eliminates giardia.

Hypothermia is the lowering of the core body temperature to below 95 degrees F (35 degrees C), usually caused by prolonged exposure to cold and characterized by drowsiness, loss of judgment or coordination, slurred speech, uncontrolled shivering, cool and pale skin, and slowed pulse and breathing. *Prevention*: avoid prolonged exposure to cold; put on extra layers of clothing and the jacket, heavy sweater or sweatshirt you brought along—before you feel cold.

Sore leg muscles are a distinct possibility if you take the walks and hikes that we recommend. *Prevention*: start a conditioning regimen two or three weeks before you get to Colorado; fast-walk 30 minutes or more every day, if your physical condition permits.

Sunburn is another familiar vacation spoiler. *Prevention*: wear a wide-brim hat, apply sunscreen and wear long sleeves and pants. And don't forget to wear those sunglasses! Potentially harmful ultra-violet rays are particularly strong at high elevations.

Ticks are abundant in early spring and summer. Some of them carry diseases such as Colorado Tick Fever and Rocky Mountain Spotted Fever. *Prevention*: when hiking or walking through undergrowth, tuck your pant legs into your socks, treat clothing with insect repellent, and check daily for ticks. To remove an embedded tick, pull it out gently with tweezers, removing all head and neck parts to prevent infection.

Wildlife, especially black bears, elk, deer, and bighorn sheep, can be dangerous. *Prevention*: photograph all wildlife from a safe distance and do not feed them. In Rocky Mountain National Park, a $50 fine may be issued to anyone who feeds or disturbs wildlife.

Here are some telephone numbers that may come in handy:

911 is an emergency number that you can dial anywhere in Colorado. It will connect you with the nearest sheriff or police department. In Rocky Mountain National Park, you can call either 911 or 970-586-1399.

Road Conditions: 303-639-1111 (Denver and west; recording) or 303-639-1234 (Denver and east; recording)

Weather: 303-398-3964 (National Weather Service, Aurora, CO.; recording).

Geography, Weather, Facts, History and Visitor Centers

Some Facts

The most outstanding feature of Colorado is its mountains (pun intended). In fact, three quarters of all land in the U.S. above 10,000 feet is within the borders of Colorado! The state has 880 mountains above 11,000 ft. and 53 over 14,000 ft. Mt. Elbert, southwest of Leadville, is the tallest at 14,433; it is 14th among the U.S.' "fourteeners." The uplift of Colorado's mountains is a result of earth's subterranean plates colliding about 65 million years ago.

The average elevation within Colorado is 6,800 ft., which makes it the highest of the 50 states. Most of that elevation is, of course, in the central mountain area, but the other two areas are what bring up the average. The eastern high plains range in elevation from 4,000 to 6,000 ft. And the western side of the state ranges from 5,000 to 10,000 ft.; it's part of the Colorado Plateau, which extends into New Mexico, Arizona, Utah and Wyoming.

Colorado is eighth among the states in total land area and 26th in population. Most of its population is clustered where the plains meet the Front Range of the mountains. Population centers include Colorado Springs and Pueblo in the south, and the Denver metropolitan area, Boulder, Fort Collins and Greeley in the north. More than 21 million acres of the state's land is forested.

Commercially, Colorado's principal industries are manufacturing, government, tourism, agriculture, aerospace, and electronics equipment. Cattle, wheat and hay are the principal livestock and agricultural products.

The state has about 310 days of sunshine per year. When you combine the sunshine and mild climate with the spectacular scenery, recreational opportunities and fascinating history, is it any wonder that Colorado is one of the most desirable vacation destinations in the United States and the world?

More Facts

- *Colorado:* A Spanish word meaning "ruddy" or "red" (the State was named for the Colorado River)
- *Nickname:* The Centennial State (admitted on August 1, 1876)
- *Population:* 4.3 million
- Capitol: Denver, the "Mile High City" (2000 Census: 554,600)

- *Land Area:* 104,091 square miles
- *Animal:* Rocky Mountain Bighorn Sheep
- *Bird:* Lark Bunting
- *Flower:* Rocky Mountain Columbine (white and lavender)
- *Tree:* Colorado Blue Spruce
- *Time Zone:* Mountain
- *State Fair:* August, in Pueblo
- *Website:* www.colorado.com

Key Historical Events

- *About 1AD-1400:* The Anasazi occupied their cliff dwellings in southwestern Colorado.
- *1706:* The territory was claimed for Spain by Juan de Ulibarri.
- *1700's:* The Spanish explored from Mexico.
- *1803:* The U.S. acquired eastern Colorado as part of President Jefferson's Louisiana Purchase. (The central portion was obtained in 1845 with the admission of Texas as a state, and the western part was acquired in 1848 as a result of the Mexican-American War.)
- *1806-1807:* U.S. Army Capt. Zebulon M. Pike explored the area; Pikes Peak is named for him. (Other government explorers followed: Maj. Stephen H. Long, Lt. John C. Fremont and Capt. John W. Gunnison.)
- *1830's:* Trappers searched for beaver and penetrated the mountains. Among them were the Bent brothers, Ceran St. Vrain, Jim Bridger, Jim Baker, Uncle Dick Wootton, Kit Carson and Louis Vasquez.
- *1833-34:* Bent's Fort (a fortified civilian trading post on the Santa Fe Trail) was built near present-day La Junta. Fort Garland, a government military post near present-day Alamosa, was operational from 1858-1883.
- *1851:* The first permanent white settlement, San Luis, was founded.
- *July, 1858*: Placer gold was discovered by Green Russell and his party of Georgians along dry creek near present-day Denver, starting Colorado's gold rush.
- *May 6, 1859:* The first gold vein was discovered near Central City by John H. Gregory.
- *February 28, 1861:* Colorado Territory was formed; President Lincoln appointed William Gilpin the first governor.
- *1869:* The conflict with the Plains Indians (Cheyenne and Arapaho) ended. (It continued with the mountain-inhabiting Ute until 1879).
- *1870:* Railways were completed to the territory.
- August 1, 1876: Colorado became the 38th state.

- *1860's through the 1890's:* Gold and silver were mined on a grand scale in Central City, Georgetown, Leadville, Breckenridge, Aspen, Cripple Creek and other locations.

Visitor Centers and Chambers of Commerce

- *Breckenridge Activity Center*, 203 S. Main St., Breckenridge, CO 80424; 970-453-5579, 877-864-0868, *www.gobreck.com.*
- *Buena Vista Chamber of Commerce*, PO Box 2021, 343 Hwy. 24 S., Buena Vista, 81211; 719-395-6612, *www.buenavistacolorado.org.*
- *Colorado Springs Visitor Information Center*, 515 S. Cascade, Colorado Springs, CO 80903; 719-635-7506, 800-888-4748, *www.experiencecoloradosprings.com.*
- *Colorado Tourism Office*, 1625 Broadway, Denver 80202, 800-265-6723, *www.colorado.com.*
- *Cripple Creek Welcome Center*, P.O. Box 430, Cripple Creek, CO; 877-858-GOLD, *www.cripple-creek.co.us.*
- *Denver Visitors Bureau*, 1555 California St., Suite 300, Denver 80202; 303-892-1112, *www.denver.org.*
- *Estes Park Chamber and Information Center*, 500 Big Thompson Ave., Estes Park, CO 80517; 970-586-4431, 800-378-3708, *www.estesparkresort.com.*
- *Georgetown Gateway Visitor Center,* PO Box 426, 404 6th St., Georgetown, CO 80444; 303-569-2555, 888-569-1130, *www.town.georgetown.co.us.*
- *Leadville/Lake County Chamber of Commerce*, PO Box 861, 809 Harrison Ave., Leadville, 80461; 719-486-3900, 888-532-3845, *www.leadvilleusa.com.*
- *Vail Valley Chamber & Tourism Bureau,* 100 E. Meadow Dr., Suite 34, Vail, 81657; 970-476-1000, 800-653-4523, *www.visitvailvalley.com.*

If You Have Kids Along

We defer to Doris Kennedy who is a true expert on this topic. A Colorado resident, she has written *Fun With the Family in Colorado* (see Selected Readings). We recommend that you purchase her book for its details and use it along with ours. You'll notice that most of the activities that we've chosen for our tour are also listed in her book. *In other words, just bring the kids along; they'll enjoy the entire tour!*

Doris recommends the following activities for kids in or near each of our tour's main stopping points:

Denver

- Colorado State Capitol Building
- Denver Art Museum
- Denver Mint
- Denver Museum of Nature and Science
- Denver Zoo
- Six Flags Elitch Gardens Amusement Park
- Museum of Miniatures, Dolls and Toys
- Ocean Journey
- Wings Over the Rockies Air and Space Museum

Boulder

- National Center for Atmospheric Research
- Celestial Seasonings
- Leanin' Tree Museum of Western Art

Golden

- Colorado Railroad Museum
- Buffalo Bill Memorial Museum and Grave
- Genesee Buffalo Herd Overlook

Morrison

- Tiny Town
- Dinosaur Ridge
- Red Rocks Park and Amphitheater

Westminster

- Butterfly Museum and Insect Center

Estes Park

- Rocky Mountain National Park
- Enos A. Mills Cabin
- Colorado Wilderness Sports (inside climbing wall)
- Hi Country Stables and SK Ltd.
- Rooftop Rodeo (mid-July)

Georgetown

- Georgetown Loop Railroad
- Lebanon Silver Mine Tour

Fairplay

- South Park City Museum

Vail

- Gondolas at LionsHead and Vail Village
- Piney River Ranch Stables
- Vail Valley Rodeo (Edwards)

Leadville

- National Mining Hall of Fame
- Leadville, Colorado & Southern Railroad
- Tabor Opera House

Cripple Creek

- Mollie Kathleen Gold Mine
- Cripple Creek & Victor Narrow Gauge Railroad
- Mueller State Park

Florissant

- Florissant Fossil Beds National Monument
- Hornbek Homestead

Cañon City

- Royal Gorge Canyon and Bridge
- Buckskin Joe (gold mining camp replica)
- Royal Gorge Scenic Railway and Museum
- Dinosaur Depot and Garden Park Fossil Area

Manitou Springs

- Cave of the Winds

- Manitou Cliff Dwellings Museum
- Miramont Castle

Colorado Springs

- U.S. Air Force Academy
- Garden of the Gods
- Rock Ledge Historic Site
- Flying W Ranch
- Pro Rodeo Hall of Fame and Museum of the American Cowboy
- Olympic Training Center
- Children's Museum of Colorado Springs
- Santa's Workshop and North Pole
- Pikes Peak Highway
- Pikes Peak Cog Railway
- Ghost Town
- North Cheyenne Canyon Park
- Seven Falls
- Cheyenne Mountain Zoo
- May Natural History Museum of the Tropics

Selected Readings

If you're like most travelers, and have the time, you may want to read some about Colorado before you leave home. With that in mind, we've compiled a short list of carefully selected books that you may enjoy and/or find useful. You can find them at *www.amazon.com*, *www.bn.com* (Barnes & Noble), your local library, or in the travel section of your favorite bookstore.

Historical Books

If you'd like to learn more about Colorado's history and people, here are some books that we've particularly enjoyed.

- ***Centennial***, by James A. Michener, Ballantine Books, New York, NY, 1983. A powerful historical novel, which will give you, a good feel for the land and its people. If you're not into geology or prehistoric animals, skim the first 100 pages or so.
- ***Colorado!***, by Dana Fuller Ross, Bantam Books, New York, NY, 1981. Another good historical novel.
- ***A Colorado History***, by Carl Ubbelohde, Maxine Benson & Duane A. Smith, Pruett Publishing Company, Boulder, CO, 2001. Fact-filled, but interesting and highly readable—as for the layman, not the student.
- ***Colorado: A Bicentennial History***, by Marshall Sprague, W.W. Norton & Company, New York, NY, 1984. Straight history, but highly readable, interesting and entertaining.
- ***A Lady's Life in the Rocky Mountains***, by Isabella L. Bird, University of Oklahoma Press, Norman, OK, 1976 (first published in London in 1879). A fascinating and beautifully written first-hand account by an English lady who visited Estes Park and nearby sites in the autumn and early winter of 1873 during her solo, round-the-world trek.

Travel Books

Here are some books that will enhance your Colorado travel experience and help you plan side trips.

- ***The Updated Colorado Guide***, by Bruce Caughey and Dean Winstanley, Fulcrum Publishing, Golden, CO, 2005. A comprehensive travel guide with excellent descriptions of major attractions, festivals and events, outdoor activities, museums and galleries, scenic drives and historical events. Selected accommodations, restaurants and local services. *If we were to purchase only one travel book about Colorado, this would be it.*

- ***Colorado Handbook***, by Stephen Metzger, Avalon Travel Publishing, Emeryville, CA, 2002. Another comprehensive guide, nicely embellished with photographs and maps.
- ***Scenic Driving Colorado,*** by Stewart M. Green, Falcon, Helena, MT, 2003. Contains maps, photographs and details on 30 of Colorado's most scenic drives. Full of side trip ideas, if you plan to extend your trip to Colorado.
- ***Colorado Travel Smart,*** by Dianna Litvak, John Muir Publications, Santa Fe, NM, 1999. Also a travelogue, the chapters are arranged in geographic sequence, so travelers can drive from one area to the next and thereby cover most of the state in 14 days.
- ***Frommer's Colorado***, by Eric Peterson, Hungry Minds, Inc., New York, NY, 2007. A comprehensive and functional travel guide containing information about attractions, lodging, restaurants, entertainment, excursions and shopping.
- ***Fun With the Family in Colorado***, by Doris Kennedy, Globe Pequot Press, Old Saybrook, CT, 2005. Wonderful companion book to ours, if you have kids along.
- ***Mobil Travel Guide: Southwest 2006***, ExxonMobil Travel Publications, Publications International, Lincolnwood, IL. Describes some accommodations listed in this book, activities, and restaurants. Also, search *http://mobiltravelguidehowstuffworks.com.*
- ***Tour Book: Colorado & Utah***, American Automobile Association; contains details on AAA's recommended accommodations listed in this book. Also, search *www.aaa.com.*
- ***Woodall's Western America Campground Directory***, ***2007*** contains details on the campgrounds listed in this book, plus much more. Also, search Woodall's website at *www.woodalls.com* for more detailed information.

Also by Bill and Celia Ginnodo

Seven Perfect Days in Northern California: A Guided Driving Tour

Their books can be viewed at

www.pridepublications.com
www.amazon.com (United States)
www.amazon.ca (Canada)
www.amazon.co.uk (United Kingdom)
www.bn.com (Barnes & Noble)
www.borders.com (Borders)

You'll find links to most of the tour's attractions and establishments at

www.pridepublications.com

Learn about the authors at

www.pridepublications.com

We would appreciate your feedback

Was this seven-day tour everything that you hoped for? Are there things that should be improved in future printings? Please contact us at *ginnodo@pridepublications.com*, 847-398-6212 (phone), 847-398-0670 (fax), or 4 N. Wilshire Lane, Arlington Heights, IL 60004